T0197235

Heroines
of
African American Golf

The Past, The Present and The Future

M. Mikell Johnson, Ph.D.

Order this book online at www.trafford.com
or email orders@trafford.com

Most Trafford titles are also available at major online book retailers.

Printed in the United States of America.

ISBN: 978-1-4269-3419-3 (sc)
ISBN: 978-1-4269-3420-9 (hc)
ISBN: 978-1-4269-3421-6 (ebk)

Library of Congress Control Number: 2010908820

*Our mission is to efficiently provide the world's finest, most comprehensive book publishing
service, enabling every author to experience success. To find out how to publish your book, your
way, and have it available worldwide, visit us online at www.trafford.com*

Trafford rev. 9/20/2010

 www.trafford.com

North America & international
toll-free: 1 888 232 4444 (USA & Canada)
phone: 250 383 6864 ♦ fax: 812 355 4082

CONTENTS

Dedication ix

Acknowledgements xi

Foreword xv

Introduction xvii

Part One
Being The First Was Not Easy

1. Wake Robin Golf Club 3
   Helen Webb Harris 3

2. Afro-American Golfers Hall of Fame 13
   Anna Mae Robinson 13

3. The Fantastic Five - Women Champions 19
   Marie Thompson Jones 21
   Lucy Williams Mitchum 25
   Thelma McTyre Cowans 32
   Ann Moore Gregory 38
   Ethel Powers Funches 45

Part Two
Changing the Scene

1. A Rare Pair 55
   Vernice Turner 57
   Madelyn Turner 61

2. The Revolutionists. 65
   Maggie Hathaway 67
   Althea Gibson 72

3. The LPGA Master Teaching Professional. 77
   Carrie Purnell Russell. 79

Photograph Gallery

Part Three
The Present

1. The Ladies Professional Golf Association (LPGA) 105

2. Why I Play Golf 109
   Paula Pearson-Tucker 109

3. I Am Still A Champion. 113
   Carrie Jones 113

Part Four
The Future

1. The Collegiate Realm 119
   Shasta Averyhardt. 123
   Jocelyn Lewis 129
   Erica Pressley 137

2. The Juniors 143
   Shelley Williams. 147
   Naomi Mitchell 152

Part Five
The Dilemma

1. Trying to Make it to the LPGA Tour 169
2. The Solution 175

Part Six
A New Beginning

1. The Athletes 187
2. The Women's Golf Organizations 197

Part Seven
Herstory

1. Achievements 212
2. Halls of Fame 219
3. The Legacy 223
Bibliography 229
Index 233

DEDICATION

This endeavor is dedicated to the African American women and child prodigy who responded to my requests to tell about their experiences in the sport of golf. These ladies did not hesitate to welcome me, a stranger, into their homes and lives to reveal the true meaning of the phrase - African American Heroines of the past, the present and the future.

Shasta Averyhardt
Carrie Jones
Jocelyn Lewis
Naomi Mitchell
Paula Pearson-Tucker
Erica Pressley
Carrie Purnell Russell
Darlene Stowers
Vernice Harris Turner
Madelyn Turner
Shelley Williams

They gave me the strength to continue and not to be discouraged.

"You can make it happen. You can help perpetuate the future of the African American woman's dream in golf."

ACKNOWLEDGEMENTS

I wish that there was a word to express one's thanks and beyond. I have met various people on my journey through the annals of history. Some have been so kind and forthcoming that the only way I can express my gratitude is to say "Thank You Plus!"

I want to thank all of the African American women who had the courage to stand on the first tee and say here "I am, today, tomorrow and in the future."

A special 'Thank You', is to be given to the golf organizations which responded to the request for information. The Lady Drivers, Les Birdies, Ridgewood Ladies, Sisters Across America and Tee Divas and Tee Dudes did not hesitate to heed the call.

Mrs. Carrie Purnell Russell, the world traveler and golf instructor, made time for me to interfere with her normal schedule.

Mrs. Winifred Stanford, the Historian of the Wake Robin Golf Club is always there for me whenever I encounter a problem.

Ms. Debert Cook, Publisher of the *African American Golfer's Digest* who inspires me to continue to look for the history.

Ms. Anna Bowman, who lends a helping hand in the time of need.

Mrs. Vernice Turner and her daughters Janet Hughes and Madelyn Turner welcomed me into their lives without question. They provided me with so much of the history of women in the United Golfers Association era.

Ms. Veronica Ragland, the great-grand niece of Julia Siler for making contact to share information about her aunt.

Ms. Rose Mary Spriggs, who always responded to my many requests.

Ms. Victoria Romero, the great-grand niece of Lucy Williams Mitchum, who wanted to share the life of her aunt.

Mr. Gregg Averyhardt, for keeping me informed as to the progress of Shasta.

The Dennis Williams' family for making sure that Shelley's contribution was hand delivered.

The Shonn Mitichell family, parents of Naomi Mitchell, who were most responsive to various requests

Mr. Michael Riddick, the Los Angeles photographer who went on a mission to locate the vintage photographs of Maggie Hathaway.

Mr. William Billingsley, Director of the National Afro-American Museum & Cultural Center, Wilberforce, OH.

Ms. Naimah Jabali-Nash, who was able to obtain the photograph of the Helen Webb Harris family.

The family of Mr. Walter Combs, grandson of Helen Webb Harris, is special because they shared precious family heirlooms.

Mr. William "Puggy" Blackmon, Director of Golf and Ms. Marci Saltzman of Golf Operations at the University of South Carolina, were most helpful in making sure that I was able to contact Erica Battle Pressely.

Mr. Scott Walker, owner/director of the SunCoast Professional Golf Tour, Orlando FL who responded to my call for his help.

Mr. Randall Burger, for recovering photographs of Lucy Williams Mitchum.

Ms. Exie Shackelford-Ochier, who provided the photographs of Ann Gregory and Thelma Cowans.

The following information specialists continued to give their assistance and valuable time to ensure that this project was completed.

Ms. Nancy Stulack, Museum & Archives Register, United States Golf Association (USGA), Far Hills NJ, provided the golf records of Althea Gibson and Ann Gregory.

Ms. JoEllen El Bashir, Curator of Manuscripts, Moorland-Spingarn Research Center at Howard University, Washington DC is always on call for the queries.

Ms. Deborah L. Yerkes, Assistant Documents Librarian, Thomas Cooper Library, University of South Carolina, Columbia SC has become my documents guru.

Ms. Vera Hooks, Periodicals Librarian, Fayetteville State University NC.

Mrs. Margaret Cox, Ms. Rebecca Drefs, Ruth Kilgallon, Margaret Collar and Elizabeth Caldwell, Librarians at the Drs. Bruce & Lee Foundation Library, Florence SC for their patience in helping me unravel the mysteries of personal data of the United Golfers Association women golfers.

Dr. Ruth Hodges, Reference & Information Specialist, and Assistant Professor at Miller F. Whittaker Library, S. C. State University, Orangeburg SC, never refused to assist in locating documentation for this research endeavor.

Ms. Lisa D. Mickey, Communications Manager, Duramed FUTURES Tour was most helpful in providing and reviewing information for the manuscript. All aspiring professional women golfers should read her articles to find out what is in store for them on the tours.

Suzy Folk has befriended me in various ways. She has been the most supportive in encouraging me to continue the story of the African American woman golfer.

The members of the Traces Women's Association tolerated my absences on Saturdays. They did allow me to win their "one putt" money when I did show up.

The following people exceeded the support that is privileged in a client and provider relationship -

Ms. Tiffany Jones, Mr. Roger Lawson, Ms. Kisha Jones, Ms. Yvonne Malone, Ms. Elizabeth Quarterman and Ms. Crystal Holiday are the document specialists who responded to the many requests.

Mr. Joseph Carney is the best photographic magician. He was able to make all of the pictures and photographs look good.

I owe a special debt of gratitude to Mrs. Sara Hough, a friend and confidante during all of these endeavors to be an author.

Jamie Michele Reid has helped me to reestablish my niche in society, especially with coaching me to be more patience and in developing a better sense of diplomacy.

Marian, I will always miss you and I know that you are watching and laughing as I attempt to correct all of the mistakes in this manuscript.

Mom, thanks for being there whenever I needed a friend and especially, a HUG.

MMJ

FOREWORD

UNITED WE STAND

Throughout history, women across the globe have always known when and how to come together, unite their energy and with persistent determination make their needs recognized. From the rights of land ownership, education and voting, women in America have firmly stood their ground until they saw legislation passed and government funding created for efforts and programs that would better serve their life situation and interests.

Now, we turn to golf. The disappointment here is that after years of finally having the legal opportunity for inclusion and participation in the game we are lacking in actualization. There are a few things that are left to be said about the need for African American women to return to playing on the LPGA Tour.

Our black women today are stronger, healthier, more educated, well traveled and living longer than ever before. They have purses, backpacks, tote bags and brief cases filled with extensive, well thought-out business plans, player projection strategies, golf equipment and clothing catalogues. They know how to walk, talk and look the part of a professional golfer. And, even more of them have impressive credentials, certifications, academic and professional training, rigorous exercise and practice regimens. These are all the right tools that are needed to play successfully on a professional field. But, what is missing is the most vital part of any golfer's playing portfolio: Sponsorship.

Actually, where I come from, there is no such thing as defeat. It is all about lessons learned. My greatest accomplishment in life has been living and breathing this entire mortal experience. Yet, to think that today, I – an African American woman and publisher of the oldest African American golf publication in America – would be unable to report on the playing statistics or winning highlights of an African American woman golfer on the LPGA Tour between the pages of my publication is almost more than I can bear. How could this happen? What in the name of God has brought this upon us? Are we loosing a war where so many battles were already won?

This is the world we live in. A world we have adapted to and modified for our own needs for the millennium. We have rallied for change of everything from environmental practices, to right-to-life laws, seeking to better ourselves as women. So, with each golf season, we are constantly reminded that it is our responsibility to make a difference in this game, to unite for the causes we strongly believe in and bring our talented black women golfers again to the forefront.

As we stand on courses across America dressed to play, we must consider the financial and mental differences our ladies are facing in making it to the Tour. We must not stand on the sidelines, satisfied, waiting for the next black woman golfer to raise herself up among us. It is just too much to ask, and a feat that no other professional Tour player has had to enact.

Together, we must unite and help our African American women return to playing on the LPGA Tour.

Debert C. Cook, CMP
Publisher
African American Golfer's Digest

INTRODUCTION

The purpose of the *Heroines of African American Golf* is to communicate the personal narratives of several athletes who have been identified as the "firsts" in their golf accomplishments. A few women, collegians and youngsters are willing to share their stories. Several women champions from United Golfers Association years are also included to provide a historical perspective for the *HEROINES* because they were truly the legendary "firsts."

The title HEROINE was chosen because it is the counterpart of HERO. The HEROINE is described as a daring person, good person, adventurous person, famous person, ideal person, legendary person, victorious person, courageous person, a role model and finally a goddess. The African American woman golfer personifies all of these traits and more. She is the woman of no equal in the days of modern sports. She is the only woman in the sport of golf who does not have an individual national United States Golf Association Championship trophy or LPGA Tour Championship trophy on her mantle. The following pages describe the adventures of heroines of the past, the present and the future.

The idea to form a women's golf club came to a school teacher, Helen Webb Harris, as she attended a social for the Royal Golf Club for men. She communicated the idea to several of her friends and they agreed to meet to discuss the possibilities of executing such an enormous and revolutionary, yet brilliant concept. The pioneering 13 women are HEROINES because they are the catalyst of a movement to establish the first African American female golf club in America – the Wake Robin Golf Club For Negro Women.

The 13 women had the audacity to challenge the all male club venues that were established by the United Golfers Association as well as white America. They were exposed to much ridicule, but, performed so well in their endeavors to be invited into the membership of the prestigious all male golf associations. Another major milestone was the election of Wake Robin members as officers and delegates of the United Golfers Association and the Eastern Golf Association to represent them in many of the sport and political affairs.

The unique independence and administrative skills of the Wake Robin Golf Club has been a developmental module for the creation of many African American women's golf clubs throughout the nation. Helen Webb Harris and her formidable 12 were the first and their courage to expose and teach women about the sport of golf will be everlasting.

One woman had the nerve to confront the United Golfers Association as to how they were handling the performance records of the Negro golfers. She is a HEROINE because she was able to persuade the organization to consider a Hall of Fame. Anna Mae Black Robinson of the Chicago Women's Golf Club was the HEROINE.

She was instrumental in forming the Chicago Women's Golf Club which became the first all female club to sponsor a United Golfers Association male tournament. She had also achieved a reputation for preserving records to be archived.

The "Fantastic Five" are HEROINES because they had the courage to be adventuresome and explore a sport that the male chauvinists had indicated that they were not welcomed or worthy to play the game. The "Fantastic Five" went on to win more United Golfers Association National Open tournaments than the most experienced male golfers. Between the times of 1930 to 1980, five amateur women dominated the United Golfers Association National Open Championship tournament scene –

The Fantastic Five

Marie Thompson Jones, 1930 – 1941
Lucy Williams Mitchum, 1932- 1946
Thelma McTyre Cowans, 1947 – 1960
Anne Moore Gregory, 1945 – 1970
Ethel P. Funches, 1954 – 1980

Many other women became lucky and knocked a champion off of her pedestal, but the victory would only be temporary. Usually the champion would return to her place of honor and dominance within a year or two.

The women formed a bond and traveled all over the country from venue to venue. They were friends, and fierce competitors, yet they remained as part of a cohesive family. At least most of them relished belonging to a golf family.

Their positive bonding was essential in a male dominated sport. The women were not welcomed in the game. This was a sport that men could enjoy without women hanging about and annoying them.

However, some clubs did not mind having the women play with the men. Often the men and women would pair up as teams to have competitive matches with clubs in other cities. One such club was the Pioneer Club in Chicago. Another was the New Amsterdam Club in New York City.

Eventually, the women gathered up enough courage to demand a place on the golf courses. Soon the tension eased as women began to compete against each other in local and regional tournaments. The Coup de Grace came in 1930 when women were allowed to play in the United Golfers Association National Open tournament. Even the 'Brown Bomber," Joe Louis, would not allow women to play in his tournaments. He was an avid proponent of equality in the golf arena, for men. Yet, he denied the equality of women of his own race to play in the sport. Finally, after eight years of the Joe Louis Open Invitational, women were permitted to play in 1946.

It is possible that the Professional Golf Association (PGA) used this behavior as a basis to keep the 'Negro' male off of their tour with – "how can you demand to play with white golfers when you do not even want to play with your own 'Negro' women?" What logical explanation can one give to justify this lopsided racial and sexual bias?

Women golfers made an immense impact on the United Golfers Association tour. They proved that they were athletes, knew how to play the game and were adept in the administrative services that seem to boggle the minds of some of the most erudite men. Afterwards many male specific clubs began to entice women to become members. This gave a club leverage when it came time to compete in the local and regional tournaments. The clubs began to boast about which had the best female players.

THAT WAS IN THE PAST

During the transition from the past to the present, there were a group of women who effected change in the game of golf for all women.

A mother and her daughter are hailed as HEROINES because the mother dared to challenge the United Golfers Association on the rules of a caddy. It was unheard of to have a teenager carry a golfer's bag and totally unusual for the teenager to be a girl. This pairing won two United Golfers Association National Open Women's Championships. Vernice Turner from a community in southern New Jersey, put the Atlantic City suburbs on the golf map by winning two National Women's Championships with her daughter, Madelyn on the bag. They write about their time playing golf in the United Golfers Association championship tournaments.

Two women can be described as revolutionists because they demanded change. These two women are hailed as HEROINES because they were rebellious in spirit, but focused on the agenda of getting things done. They were polar opposites, one was a budding actress and the other a fierce athlete, yet they had one thing in common that was to create a change in the work place and athletics. Their agenda was that there can not be a "separate, but equal program" to bring about equality in a democracy.

The aspiring actress spent her life trying to make things right as to race relations. She is a HEROINE because she endured a lot of criticism for her efforts, but, had made the commitment to effect a change in the film industry and on the golf courses. Her name is Maggie Hathaway.

A tennis star became a HEROINE because she was a famous sports personality who dared to be different. She pushed the envelope in two sports and was not afraid to show her mettle. In the 1960s a woman athlete, who had played golf as part of a Sports Management and Physical Education requirement at Florida A & M College announced that she was going to enter the golf arena as a professional. The sports community did a double take and was amazed that the tennis legend, Althea Gibson had made the most puzzling announcement of the 20th century.

Althea Gibson was a champion's champion. She did not make excuses for her failures nor did she back down from poor performances. Although she never won on the LPGA or USGA tours, she made her presence known and unforgettable.

Then, there is the high school teacher who is a HEROINE because she became enamored with the sport of golf. She took the sport to the youth of Japan, to the youth on the U. S. Army bases, and finally, to the youth of Maryland. She taught the youth about the beauty of the sport and how to enjoy it. Carrie P. Russell traveled from the United States to Japan and infected the love of golf among the youth from the Orient to the United States. In 1971, she became the first African American LPGA Certified Golf Instructor. She brought the sport of golf to the youth as a friend, as a coach and as one who believed that all it takes is to care and be responsible as the youth find their way. Her passion for the sport can be felt as she takes us on a journey around the world.

THAT WAS DURING THE TRANSITION YEARS

Today, there is not one African American female golfer on the premiere women's tours in the world –

> the Ladies Professional Golf Association,
> the Asian Ladies Golf Association,
> the European Ladies Golf Association

The African American women who now play on the Duramed FUTURES tour and those who have played in the past are HEROINES because of their willingness to make an attempt to go to the "next level" of competition. They followed a yellow brick road to find if there was really a wizard at the end to turn their efforts into the magical top five as year end finalists. Their presence on the tour has encouraged more neophytes to enter the sport as a career. The youngsters now view the developmental tours with optimism and can visualize a chance for success at the end of the road.

There are many African American women who are very capable of playing tournament golf. They are playing and have played excellent collegiate golf. So, where are they now?

Most of them have chosen not to participate in golf as a career path. Many of them have made the decision to become involved in a legitimate professional career where they can earn reliable financial stability with perks.

The LPGA and their developmental FUTURES tour are desperately looking for African American women golfers to ascend to the level of competitive tour golf and make their presence known. Though they applaud the ones who make the qualifying school, they are also seeking the ones who want to make golf a career at the highest level. They are looking for women who want to win and maintain a position in contention at each and every tournament. They want many African American women champions.

Lisa Mickey, Communications Officer of the Duramed FUTURES Tour has indicated that the best experience for a rookie is to play on the FUTURES tour for at least a year to acclimate to the demands of a tour. She is correct in her assessment, but unless a rookie has a solid financial base, the exposure on the FUTURES tour can also be a waste of time and effort. Sometimes it is best to get a real job, and play golf with corporate clients.

There are still several African American women, who are not giving up. Despite their financial circumstances, they have committed themselves to following a dream. Athletes like Darlene Stowers, Tierra Manigault, Loretta Lyttle and Paula Pearson-Tucker are prime examples of people who have struggled to exist in the game over the years. They have not advanced to the LPGA tour yet, but have the courage to continue to try. Still, at this moment in time, the sport of golf is their first priority. Paula Pearson-Tucker tells why she is still playing golf on the Duramed FUTURES Tour.

There are not many women who are alive today who played during the United Golfers Association era. Carrie Jones, the 1962 United Golfers Association National Open Women's Champion, makes a comparison as to her experiences during the years of segregation and the present.

There are fewer women who had exposure on the LPGA and/or the FUTURES tours. So, is there a chance for an African American female to break through and become a contender on these tours?

THESE ARE THE CIRCUMSTANCES OF THE PRESENT

Someone is out there who will appear in the future and take the golf world on a historic journey that will expose and solve the dilemma of African American women in professional golf.

The African American woman has eliminated herself from the LPGA playing fields since 1995. Not one African American woman has managed to meet the qualifications to obtain the elusive LPGA membership card via the "Qualifying School," the Duramed FUTURES Tour, Sponsors' exemption or as a "Monday "qualifier. And, now we are fast approaching a milestone of 15 years or more without an African American woman as a playing professional on the LPGA tour.

However, it is amazing that there are two nationally known African American women who have achieved success and are well recognized within the golf community for their contributions to the game. They are Barbara Douglas and Renee Powell. They are considered as the current recognizable African American standard bearers and are often solicited to represent diversity within the sport.

Renee Powell, a former tour player, has received various accolades from the LPGA and PGA tours, and is active with the First Tee Program of the World Golf Foundation. Whereas, Barbara Douglas has been a guiding force of the National Minority Golf Foundation and is still extremely active with the USGA.

Their accomplishments have transcended the "diversity stigma" because they are no longer referred to as - "the First African American women who…" They are recognized as contributors to the entire spectrum of the sport over the past 15 to 20 years. They have persevered in administrative positions where many other women had given up.

Their successful examples have certainly encouraged the development of the "new breed" and highly motivated collegiate women and teens to change the landscape of the sport. These are the ones who are demanding a chance to make it happen. Their diversity is not to just be a representative, but, to be the change agent in various roles.

WHAT DOES THE FUTURE HOLD?

Collegiate women are HEROINES for their tenacity and positive contributions toward team championships. The performance of each collegiate golfer has reinforced the slogan – there is no "I" in team. Young women like Shasta Averyhardt, Erica Battle-Pressley and Jocelyn Lewis are usually in the top ten academic categories. They have set examples for many juniors to follow. Each one of these young women reveals the importance that the sport of golf has made in their lives. One day all of them will be listed in an African American Collegiate Golf Hall of Fame for Achievements. They may not pursue golf as a career but they will have made a most positive impact on society as professionals in their chosen fields.

The junior golf HEROINES have to be admired for their long term commitment to the sport. They have selected idols and immediately start to emulate them on the golf course. In addition, the junior golfers are academically ahead of their peers at any grade level because they are determined to earn golf scholarships. The junior golfers are the most positive HEROINES because of their genuine enthusiasm. The youngsters who are competing actually "love" to play the game. The passion is still there and this makes them the "true" amateurs. If their love of the game and passion persist, they will generate a new breed of golfer. Shelley Williams and Naomi Mitchell are already exploring a future in golf.

The African American women's organizations are also HEROINES. They are exposing the sport to the community grassroots adults and children. They are encouraging females to become more active in local, regional and national golf activities, on a regular basis. The women's clubs are making their presence known nationwide.

In 2010, it will be 80 years since Marie Thompson became the first women to win an ethnic major championship. In 2010, it will be 54 years since Ann Gregory appeared in an USGA tournament. In 2010, it will be 47 years since Althea Gibson appeared on the LPGA Tour. Are we waiting for 300 years for the mystical appointed one to make an appearance? Is there any acceptable time period for the African American woman to earn her credentials to become a professional member of the LPGA tour?

An acceptable time will be when the African American community stops complaining about the lack of the athletes on the LPGA tour. And, begin to care enough to financially support the ones who are trying their best to get there.

These athletes have to be more than a good golfer. They also need to know that the basic and daily needs of living are taken care. Then they can maintain a competitive edge to become professional and earn the required credentials. The reigning professional players have only one job and that is to play golf.

The athletes of today are accepting the challenge to make it happen and win tournaments. They all have the confidence to win and the only goal is to focus on winning. They will not wait for any magic to realize their goals. And, when they do achieve stardom, in spite of us, we will be ashamed that we did not support them from the beginning.

In the meantime, I will continue to celebrate the glorification and the acknowledgement of the HEROINES of African American golf as they were in the past, as they are in the present and as they will be in the future.

Mikell Johnson

PART ONE

Being The First Was Not Easy

THE BEGINNING

We all know that being the first is not easy. It is because one is expected to establish a precedent. All eyes are watching to see if the aims and the goals are met within a reasonable amount of time. This volume would not be deemed as historical if it did not contain the contributions of the matrons of African American golf.

The following seven women are described as innovators. They wanted to make a change in the rules and regulations governing the sport of golf in favor of women. Each one had the self determination and inner strength to achieve a leadership position in the sport.

They definitely changed the sport of golf to include the accomplishments of African American women.

1. Helen Webb Harris had the foresight to persuade women to form the first golf club
2. Anna Mae Black Robinson envisioned a sanctuary for golf records and memorabilia
3. Marie Thompson Jones challenged the men for championship equality
4. Lucy Williams Mitchum was the first to win four major championships
5. Thelma McTyre Cowans was the first to claim five major championships
6. Ann Moore Gregory was known as the "Queen of Negro Golf"
7. Ethel Powers Funches is still the only woman to have won seven championship titles.

1. The Wake Robin Golf Club
Helen Webb Harris

Helen Harris who resided at 79 "R" Street, Washington DC, sent postcards to many of her friends and associates, inviting them to come to a meeting, on April 22, 1937.

Twelve women responded, out of the many invitations, to listen to a radical proposal involving golf. The attendees were Adelaide Adams, Dorothy Booth, Anna Johnson, Bernice Proctor, Hazel Foreman, Isabell Betts, Stella Skinner, Mabel Jones, Ethel Williams, Vydie Carter, Jerenia Reid, Evelyn Beam and Helen Harris.

The thirteen women initiated a gender revolution when they began to discuss the historic concept of forming a golf club exclusively for and by women. It did not take long for the revolutionaries to draft a plan, elect officers and choose a name.

They elected the usual positions of officers with the most influential responsibilities to be held and managed by Helen Harris as president and Mabel Jones as the golf instructor.

The name of the organization would be – The Wake Robin Golf Club for Negro Women. The Wake Robin Golf Club became first African American women's golf club in America. This was the first women's club organized to promote the game of golf as a primary objective for and managed by women. On April 22, 1937, the women became a symbol of liberation, emancipation and bravery to take an idea and quietly conceptualize it into a reality. The club defied all ethnic male golf organizations as to who can play golf, and, who can control the future of golf in the United States.

The objectives of the group were to:

1. give women the opportunity to learn about the sport of golf, this would entail the history of the sport, equipment, rules, scoring and tournament venues

2. provide lessons to be given by a golf instructor for women to develop the skills to play the game and to develop several golf champions

3. schedule tournaments for the women to play within the Club and to become proficient in competing against women in other geographic areas

4. initiate a similar golf program for the youth to become involved in the sport

5. perform community services, as a club, for the church, school, hospital, shelter,

6. and to be politically active in the integration of golf courses and programs

Before the Wake Robin Golf Club was a year old, it was involved in an integration claim against the United States Department of Interior. The Wake Robin Golf Club joined with the Royal Golf Club to petition the Secretary of Interior, Harold Ickes, to integrate the all white golf courses, in the DC area. Sec. Ickes opted to build a 9-holes golf course for Blacks in the Anacostia section of Washington, rather than to integrate the all white existing facilities. The 9-holes Langston Golf Course was opened with much fanfare on June 11, 1939. Although, it gave the golfers a place to hit balls, it was best described as a cow pasture with a raw sewage ditch running through it. This facility was to appease the African American golf community and to keep golf as a sport – "separate but equal."

The Wake Robin Golf Club would not let it go. They made sure that Sec. Ickes knew that they were professional women who knew that separate did not mean equal. After much pro and con negotiating, by the Wake Robin Golf Club, Sec. Ickes integrated all of the golf courses within the DC area, with a proclamation in 1941.

The present 18-holes, 145 acres Langston Golf Course was renovated and reopened in 1955. It is ironic that the PGA lifted its Jim Crow policy three years later, in 1958, to allow African American male golfers to compete in some tournaments. The Langston Golf Course was placed on the National Register of Historic Places in 1991.

The women of the Wake Robin Golf Club were quickly becoming known as the task force involved in desegregation throughout the golf communities. The Wake Robin Golf Club modules of getting things done, in an effective way, was so impressive that the male dominated United Golfers Association and the Eastern Golf Association wanted a piece of the action. These male oriented groups desperately needed administrative support to maintain corporate reigns over the myriad of individual golf clubs that spread from the East coast to the Midwestern states and from Florida to Texas.

5

The Wake Robin Club was extended an invitation to join the United Golfers Association and the Eastern Golf Association. The Wake Robin Golf Club women were approached to assist the two groups with their administrative affairs as directors on various executive boards and committees. Helen Harris was the first woman to be elected as president of the Eastern Golf Association and served two terms, 1942 to 1943 and 1943 to 1944. Another first was the election of Paris Brown as the United Golfers Association Tournament Director from 1954 to 1964 for both men and women's golf.

The Wake Robin Golf Club has continued to adhere to their primary initiatives. One in particular was to provide a training module for junior golfers to participate in the game. Today, the initiative is still viable as the Interclub Federation of Golfers Junior Golf Program. The program initiated in 1937 also served as a model for the United Golfers Association junior golf program.

Another initiative was to groom championship women golfers. The group has produced multiple local club champions, regional champions, state champions and United Golfers Association National Open Women's Champions. Some of the more recognizable multiple champions are -

Club Regional & State Champions

Sarah Smith	Ethel Terrell Downing	Hazel Foreman
Elizabeth Rice McNeal	Ethel Funches	Frances Mays
Laurie Stokien	Jean Miller Colbert	

The United Golfers Association National Open Women's Amateur Champions
Ethel Funches, 1959, 1960, 1963, 1967, 1968, 1969, 1973
Laurie Stokien, 1975
Top 2nd to 3rd place in UGA National Open Women's Amateur Championship round
Alma Arvin, 1956
Hazel Foreman, 1946, 1947, 1948
Elizabeth Mc Neal, 1959
Frances Mays, 1963
Ethel Funches, 1955, 1957, 1958, 1961

The Wake Robin Golf Club revolutionized golf for women across the vast span of the country and is still not highlighted in the history that it deserves. The Wake Robin Golf Club was finally recognized as a pioneer in the 2009 African American Golfers Hall of Fame, but there is not a plaque for the club in the World Golf Hall of Fame. Also, four Wake Robin Golf Club members were inducted into the now defunct United Golfers Association 'Afro-American Golfers Hall of Fame' -

Paris Brown, 1963   Helen Harris, 1973

Ethel Funches, 1969   Ethel Williams, 1975

The Wake Golf Club had envisioned that eventually other women's clubs would emerge all over the country. And, eventually become a part of a united and national women's golf coalition. This is the only initiative of the Wake Robin Golf Club that has not come to fruition. Perhaps the newly established women's club will adopt this initiative to become a coalition to provide an incubation system for athletes who want to elect to play tour golf as a career.

Some of the women's clubs that were influenced by the formation of the Wake Robin Golf Club during the first fifty years, between 1937 and 1987 are:

Chicago Women's Golf Club, Chicago in 1937

Vernondale/Vernoncrest Golf Club, Los Angeles in 1947

Green's Ladies Golf Club, Philadelphia in 1954

Choi-Settes Peace Golf Club, Chicago, 1960

Monumental Women's Golf Auxillary, Baltimore, 1960

Women of the Sixth City Golf Club, Cleveland, 1960

Debutantes Golf Club, Philadelphia, 1965

Ebony Ladies Golf League, Chicago, 1974

Les Birdies Golf Club of Charlotte NC, 1976

Garden State Dufferettes Golf Club, Newark NJ, 1980

Today, there are many more African American women golf organizations appearing annually because of the impact of Helen Webb Harris.

The influence of Helen Webb Harris has extended beyond 50 years. And, there is no longer a one "Black women's" golf club, but a multitude of clubs and organizations with the primary purpose of exposing and teaching African American women about the sport of golf. Helen Webb Harris is the heroic icon for African American women in golf.

Helen Webb Harris was the wife of a physician who was one of the founders of the men's Royal Golf Club in Washington DC. She was an educator in the Washington DC school system and knew how to expand the minds and souls of young people to explore the unknown. She was an idealist and dreamer who could see beyond the horizon to become a trailblazer of change.

Helen Webb Harris took the opportunity to evoke change in the lives of African American women relative to the sport of golf. She had an epiphany that materialized into a reality. She formed the first golf organization for "Colored" women with the strength, courage and support of the wives of others prominent Washington physicians. The club selected the name "Wake Robin" to epitomize their efforts. It is a plant that is strong and viable, which characterizes the persona of Helen Webb Harris and her compatriots in establishing the club.

The Helen Webb Harris Scholarship Fund was established at the 70th Anniversary in 2007. Her dream to involve African American women in the sport of golf has transcended into the 21st century. The 75th Anniversary will be celebrated in 2012.

WAKE ROBIN GOLF CLUB, ca. 1940

| Lorraine | Sara | Clara | Bonita | Paris | | Amelia | Frankie | Helen | | Hazel | Jerenia | Adelaide |
| Sawyer | Smith | Reed | Harvev | Brown | | Lucas | Watkins | Harris | | Foreman | Reid | Adams |

Wake Robin Golf Club

Members of the Wake Robin Golf Club, ca. 1940. Photograph courtesy of the Wake Robin Golf Club Archives.

Helen Harris & Family

Helen Harris with daughter Helen and Dr. Albert Harris. Photograph courtesy of Walter Combs (Grandson of Dr. & Mrs. Harris).

Helen Harris with trophy

Helen Webb Harris accepts the Washington Evening Star Newspaper winner's golf trophy, ca.1950s. Photograph courtesy of Walter Combs.

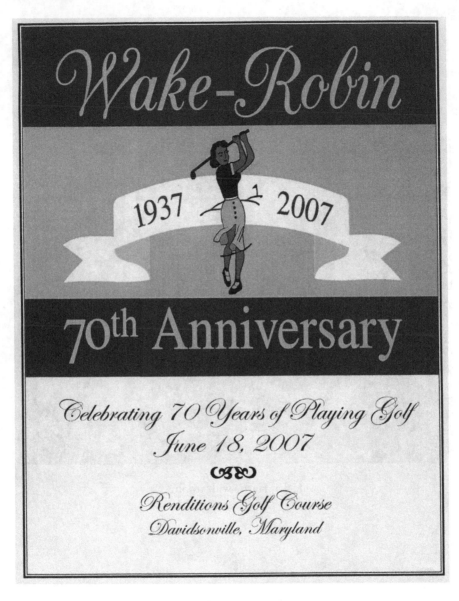

Wake Robin Program Cover

70th Anniversary Program Cover, June 18, 2007. Program Cover courtesy of the Wake Robin Golf Club Archives

2. The UGA/Afro-American Golfers Hall of Fame

Anna Mae Black Robinson

The United States Colored Golfers Association was formed in 1926. The purpose of the Association was to unify all of the individual golf groups into one powerful organization. Each group retained its own identity, but, this unification would provide structure with solidarity in governance, politics and finances for Colored golfers. The representation was divided into three geographic areas – Northeast, Southeast and Midwest districts.

In 1929, the name of the organization was changed to the United Golfers Association. The Association had solidified its membership base and was able to produce an official magazine entitled – *The United Golfer* in 1930. The magazine gave credibility to the existence of the Association. The feats of the clubs and individual players were published, as well as information on social and civil rights activities. The United Golfers Association had successfully achieved all of its goals and mandates. Included were a schedule of 15 tournaments per year and a season ending, three day Championship Tournament for Professional and Amateur golfers.

1930 was also the year that the United Golfers Association finally allowed women to participate in the Association events. Women were invited to participate in the Championship too. While all of these good things were happening for the Association, questions arose as to who was responsible for keeping the records of tournaments results and participant performances. Were the records to be kept by the host club or the district or the Association administration?

One woman came forward with a solution, after 29 years of questions and procrastination by all levels. The woman is Anna Mae Black Robinson.

Anna Mae Black Robinson established and was the first President of the Chicago Women's Golf Club. She was reelected to that position several times. She had also served in various offices within the United Golfers Association as a Vice-President, Assistant Tournament Director, and Historian. She was not a stranger to how records could be mismanaged and artifacts could be lost. She recognized the need to have a facility to house the Association's records in an archival format under the supervision of a responsible management team.

Mrs. Robinson made a proposal to the United Golfers Association executive committee that it should establish a Hall of Fame. The Hall would collect, archive and maintain the records and artifacts of the Negro golfers.

It took an extraordinary amount of time to get the proposal on the agenda for consideration because the executive committee only met every two years. Finally, after much coercion, the committee approved the proposal as worthy of consideration. The United Golfers Association Hall of Fame was officially established in 1959, on paper.

Thereafter, the Association members would gather to celebrate the selection of the honorees worthy to be in the Hall of Fame, on a yearly basis.

Anna Mae Black Robinson is definitely a heroine because she had accomplished, in a few years, what the entire United Golfers Association administration could not or would not enact in 29 years.

In 1969, Dr. Adolph Scott was appointed as the executive director/curator of the records and artifacts. Anna Robinson and Dr. Scott envisioned that the Hall of Fame would be housed at the National Afro-American Museum and Cultural Center in Wilberforce OH. Thus, the name, the UGA/National Afro-American Golfers Hall of Fame evolved.

They began to research and solicit information as to how the feat would be accomplished. Anna Robinson devoted much of her time to the project of fine tuning the wording and responsibilities of all of the parties involved. Apparently some discord developed between the Society and the UGA, but Robinson was not to be deterred. She continued to press and maintained the negotiations between several different Historical Society and UGA administrative changes.

Although, the Ohio Historical Society would provide the space, it was firm in the negotiations as to the plans, design and maintenance of the exhibit. The hopes of Robinson did not waiver, she was persistent in developing a proposal that would be acceptable to the Historical Society and the UGA executive committee.

It took almost another 20 years (1969 – 1987) before a document was deemed ready for signatures. Finally, in 1987, the <u>Memorandum of Understanding</u> was presented to both parties, The Historical Society and the United Golfers Association for the approval signatures.

The "Terms and Conditions" of the Memorandum also contained various stipulations of accountability required of the UGA –

1. Initially the UGA would provide the Ohio Historical Society with funds for the planning and design of the exhibit, which would not begin until the sum was paid.
2. The UGA would provide additional funds for the upkeep, maintenance and expenses for the exhibit.
3. The UGA would provide to the Historical Society with a plan of action for the raising of the funds for the project.

The total sum of money required was in the six digits. The document was signed by –

Gary C. Ness, Director   John E. Fleming, Director
Ohio Historical Society   National Afro-American Museum
                                and Cultural Center

The signature line for any representative of the UGA Hall of Fame committee or the UGA executive committee remained blank. There was no signature of approval for the Memorandum of Understanding by the United Golfers Association.

After several years without a compromise or a representative of the UGA signature, the expectations of establishing a Hall of Fame exhibit was abandoned in 1989.

There would not be an exhibit dedicated to the history of the Negro in the sport of golf in the near future, due to the lack of funds.

Anna Mae Black Robinson was not to relinquish her dreams and hopes that easily. She made sure that a "Historian" was appointed within the Chicago Women's Golf Club organization to archive and maintain all of the records and activities of the organization.

The majority of the memorabilia is about women as related to the many Chicago Women's Golf Club and the Mid-Western District tournaments. However, if any men entered into these designated CWGC tournaments, their records are archived.

MEMORANDUM OF UNDERSTANDING

(Proposal of Anna Mae Black Robinson, as
expanded by Dr. Adolph Scott)

"This memorandum of understanding represents the intentions, terms and conditions, and agreements between the Ohio Historical Society (Society), which operates the National Afro-American Museum and Cultural Center (Museum) and the Afro-American Golfers Association and Hall of Fame (Golfers).

INTENTIONS

The Golfers, being desirous of a relationship with the Society, do indicate their intent to support and assist Museum curatorial staff to identify and acquire artifacts and objects relative to the achievement of African-Americans in the game of golf. The Golfers do intend to provide adequate funds for the design of an appropriate exhibit, and in the event of a permanent relationship, will provide adequate funds for the maintenance, upkeep and possible upgrading of such exhibit.

It is the intent of the Society to provide such space in the Museum as will adequately and affectively display the Golfer's exhibit. And will cooperate to identify and acquire artifacts and objects illustrating the achievements of Black golfers. The Museum will maintain such exhibit according to the appropriate standards, and will cooperate with the Golfers as necessary to periodically update said exhibit.

Copy reprinted courtesy of the National Afro-
American Museum & Cultural Center, OH

3. The Fantastic Five United Golfers Association Women Champions

THE CHAMPIONS

Before 1930, the United Golfers Association National Open Championships, there were several golf clubs that catered to excellent women golfers. The women played each other and sometimes teamed with the men in golf outings. Many of the women were married to men who had learned to play in college and who used golf as a social and business outlet.

In 1930, women were ready to prove that they could play in competitive tournament events. They wanted to establish organized championship flights to vie for a title and trophy at the national level. Since that initial tournament, the Fantastic Five women continued to establish monumental "first" achievements in the history of the United Golfers Association National Open Championships.

Marie Thompson Jones of the Pioneer Golf Club in Chicago was the first to win two United Golfers Association National Open Women's Championship titles in succession.

Lucy Williams Mitchum was the first to win a total of four United Golfers Association National Open Women's titles.

Thelma McTyre Cowans was the first to obtain five United Golfers Association National Open Women's titles.

Ann Gregory was the first African American woman to play in any United States Golf Association National event.

Ethel Funches was the first to win seven United Golfers Association National Open Women's Titles.

These women won the first place United Golfers Association National Open Women's trophy 30 time in a span of 45 years, from 1930 to 1975. Thelma Cowans, Ann Gregory and Ethel Funches are the only ones, of the five women, inducted into the UGA/ Afro-American Golfers Hall of Fame.

Marie Thompson Jones - The First Champion

Marie Thompson was small in stature and could wield a driver as if it was an extension of her body. She was a member of the Chicago Pioneer Club, established by the golf icon – Walter Speedy. Marie Thompson played golf on a competitive basis with the men and was often paired with them in intercity tournament matches. When it came to golf, she was a "professional's pro."

There is no record of when Thompson took up the game of golf or when she joined the Pioneer Club. She was among the group of women in the Chicago area like Anna Mae Black, Cleo Ball, Geneva Wilson, Vivian Pitts and Lucille McKee. These women were Pioneer Club members before they established the Chicago Women's Golf Club in 1937.

Marie Thompson was the independent sort and did not join with the women to form the Chicago Women's Golf Club. She chose to remain with the Pioneer Club to coerce the United Golfers Association to admit women into their regional and national tournaments.

The United Golfers Association was formed in 1926 to bring all of the splintered golf clubs under one umbrella. The Association was divided into four geographic groups – Northeast, Eastern, Midwest and Southern golf regions. The Association began to hold the National Open Championships, for male amateurs and professionals, in 1927.

By 1930, after denying the entry of any women golfers of caliber, into the United Golfers Association National Open Championships, the Association decided to justify the reasoning for denying women – they could not perform at such a high level of competitive golf to attract golf fans. To ensure that this was correct, the Association decided to allow any woman golfer "of note" to participate in the 1930 United Golfers Association National Open Championships.

The competitive section for the women was named the "United Golfers Association National Open Women's Championship." This token inducement of a national title and a trophy brought together 16 women, nationwide, who had the courage to step forward to expose their golf games to the Negro men, the Negro press, the Negro world of doubters and most of all to the Negro women out there who were too afraid to participate.

The presence of 16 women competitors was a real shocker to the Association, since only 22 men showed up for the national tournament. Were the men intimidated by the presence of women or were the 'no shows' a sign of a boycott because of the presence of the women? If it was a boycott, the men lost, because Marie Thompson played a practice round with the men a day before the actual Open tournament.

The venue selected for this moment in history was the Casa Loma Golf Course in Wisconsin. The women in the field were Marie Thompson, Geneva Wilson, Mrs. E. Saunders, Esther Smith, Pearl Dorn, Mrs. E. G. Calvert, Mrs. T. Funches, Mrs. Leon Motts, Mrs. E. Wilson, Thelma Blanchard, Marian McGruder, Mrs. M. Nall, Mrs. C. L. Burgess, Lucy Williams, Lucille McKee and Bell Diggs. Some of the women still chose to be identified by their husband's name or initials for anonymity.

Marie Thompson knew all of the women in the field. But, she set out to prove a point that this was not going to be a friendly 18 holes match because it was all about history and to demonstrate that the women could play golf at a national tournament.

Marie Thompson beat her nearest competitor, Lucy Williams, by 16 strokes and the third place finisher, Esther Smith, by 20 shots. The consensus of opinion was that it was a fluke happening.

The second United Golfers Association National Open Women's Championship, in 1931, was held in the Chicago area at the Sunset Hills Golf Course. The women's tournament was expanded to 27 holes. The entire field of golfers consisted of 48 amateurs, 23 pros and 16 women.

Marie Thompson	Lucy Williams	Mrs. E. G. Calvert
Mrs. T. Funches	Lucille McKee	E. Saunders
Bell Diggs	Geneva Wilson	Esther Smith

Marian McGruder	M. Nall	Pearl Dorn
Mrs. C. L. Burgess	Elizabeth Grove	E. Wilson
	Thelma Blanton	

Marie Thompson was still on a mission, to show the men that the women were not an extension of the male husband/boyfriend tolerance, but a viable force to contend with in the sport of golf.

Marie Thompson of the Chicago Pioneer Golf Club defeated Lucy Williams of the Douglas Park Golf Club, Indianapolis, for the second time by 6 strokes and Elizabeth Grove of the New Amsterdam Golf Club, of New York City, by 8 strokes.

Marie Thompson had set a precedent by defending her championship title as the first and only United Golfers Association Open Women's Champion of 1930 and 1931. Her feat sent a clear message to the United Golfers Association and its male membership that women could play excellent golf and on a few occasions had a better score than the men.

Marie Thompson was the defending champion at the 1932 United Golfers Association National Women's Open. The tournament was held in Indianapolis with a field of 12 women.

Marie Thompson	Cookie Hamilton	Lucille McKee
Marian McGruder	Ada Bolton	Lucy Williams
Thelma Blanton	Cleo Halloway	Ella Able
Anna Johnson	Jennie Walker	Julia Siler

Marie Thompson was defeated by the woman who finished in second place to her twice – Lucy Williams from the Douglas Park Golf Club of Indianapolis.

Marie Thompson continued to play in the United Golfers Association National Open Women's tournaments, until 1941. Although, she never won the title again, from 1933 to 1941 she always finished in a top ten position. She finished in third place three times and finished fourth or more six times.

Marie Thompson had established a record in the history of the United Golfers Association. In 1930, the first Women's tournament, had sixteen women in the field and by 1941, there were 45 women golfers in pursuit of the championship title.

In 1936, Marie Thompson married Samuel O. Jones and set up residence in Detroit. She continued to play golf on a limited basis. She became instrumental in expanding the Detroit Amateurs Golf Association as a regional championship venue. She had won this tournament four times, during her career, in 1931, 1932, 1933 and 1941.

Marie Thompson Jones was the first woman to win back to back United Golfers Association Championship National Open titles in 1930 and 1931. Frank Gaskin was the first male amateur to win back to back United Golfers Association National Open titles in 1928 and 1929. Howard Wheeler was the first male professional to win back to back United Golfers Association National Open titles in 1946, 1947 and 1948.

Marie Jones had achieved her goal - to have women recognized as a viable component of the United Golfers Association National Open Championship structure.

Lucy Williams Mitchum - The Record Breaker

Lucy Williams was the first woman golfer to win the United Golfers Association National Open Women's Championship title four times.

Lucy Williams has no beginning and no end, as far as vital statistics are concerned. She played out of the Douglas Park Golf Club located in Indianapolis, Indiana. Some of the other notable women golfers were Ella Able, Mildred Bradley, Mildred Smith and Marjorie Cabell.

Lucy Williams was among the historical group of 16 women who petitioned the United Golfers Association to allow women to play in the 1930 National Open Championships. The women only asked for legitimate player flights, player handicaps and trophy prizes in lieu of financial remunerations since they were amateurs.

Lucy Williams placed second twice to Marie Thompson in 1930 and 1931. The breakthrough of her career in the United Golfers Association's major league was in 1932. The tournament was held in Indianapolis. Williams was in familiar surroundings. She had to compete with such golf titans as Marie Thompson, Ella Able and Julia Siler. The other women in the field were Marian McGruder, Thelma Blanton, Anna Johnson, Cookie Hamilton, Ada Bolton, Cleo Hallaway, Jennie Walker, and Lucille McKee. However, Lucy Williams was able to prevail and became the 1932 United Golfers Association National Open Women's Champion. Ironically, Marie Thompson finished in second place.

The 1933 United Golfers Association National Open was held at the Sunset Hills Golf Course, located in Chicago. Julia Siler of St. Louis won the Champion title over a field of 11 women. Lucy Williams finished in second place and Marie Thompson finished in third place.

Ella Able of the Douglas Park Golf Club, Indianapolis won the 1934 and 1935 United Golfers Association National Open Women's Championships. Lucy Williams finished in second place again. Marie Thompson finished in third place and Laura Thoroughgood, the four times winner of the Eastern Golf Association, finished in fourth place.

Lucy Williams reclaimed the United Golfers Association National Open Women's Championship Title in 1936 and defended the title in 1937. This accomplishment made her the first women to win three of the Championship titles. Only two men had won three titles before. The amateur golfer, Frank Gaskins won in 1928, 1929 and 1932. Pat Ball, the professional golfer won three titles in 1927, 1929 and 1934.

It is a blemish in African American golf history that the newspaper media did not embellish on this moment in golf achievements for women. The media dwelt on the hole by hole play of John Dendy, the professional golfer.

The 1936 United Golfers Association National Open was held at the Cobbs Creek Golf Course located in Philadelphia. Lucy Williams won the Championship. Ella Able finished in second place and Laura Thoroughgood finished in third place position. Cleo Ball, Rhoda Fowler, Vivian Pitts, Mildred Bradley, Edith Hawkins, Juanita Scott, Melnee Moye, Esther Brent and Mrs. Harris were also in the competitive field.

The 1937, United Golfers Association Open was held at the Highland Golf Course in Cleveland. This time, Aline Davis came in second to Lucy Williams. The field also included the usual big hitters such as Mary Brown, Edith Hawkins, Vivian Pitts, Mildred Bradley, Laura Thoroughood, and the contingent from the Chicago Women's Golf Club.

Lucy Williams had set the record of three wins for the United Golfers Association Open tournaments and was gearing up for her fourth win. The 1938 United Golfers Association National Open was held at Palos Park in Chicago. The field was formidable with 18 of the best women golfers like Cleo Ball, Geneva Wilson, Marie Thompson Jones, Ella Able, and Rhoda Fowler. The hopes of Lucy Williams were dashed by a young unknown from Atlanta, Georgia – Melnee Moye. The 1939 and 1940 United Golfers Association National Open Women's Championships were won by Geneva Wilson of the Chicago Women's Golf Club. In the meantime, Lucy Williams married her third husband, Russell Mitchum, who owned the Triangle Night Club in Indianapolis, They lived at 3034 N. Capitol Avenue, Indianapolis.

Forty-five women were entered in the 1941 United Golfers Association National Open tournament. The Open was held at the Ponkapoag Golf

Course in Canton, near Boston. Included in the mix was another young golfer from Atlanta, Thelma McTyre. Lucy Williams was defeated in the championship quarterfinal rounds by Marie Thompson Jones, her perennial competitor.

The victor of the 1941 Open was Cleo Ball and her friend, Vivian Pitts finished in second place. They represented the Chicago Women's Golf Club very well. The championship win by Cleo Ball was unique in that her husband, Pat Ball won the United Golfers Association Professional Open Championship.

The United Golfers Association had placed a moratorium on the National Opens. No tournaments would be held during the World War II years. The next United Golfers Association National Open would take place in 1946.

Some of the tournaments, Lucy Williams Mitchum played in during the moratorium were the –

Western Open	Mid-Western Open
Western Amateur	Indiana Open
Amateur Golf Association	Windy City Open
Sunset Hills Open	Joe Louis Open

Four years passed by before the next significant regional tournament would be opened to women in a male designated tournament. The Joe Louis Open was a tournament that was closed to women aspirants until 1946. Ann Gregory, Mildred Butkins, Laura Pierson, Aline Woods, Marjorie Cabbell, Marie Thompson Jones, Sarah Smith and Lucy Williams Mitchum were in the field.

Lucy Williams Mitchum earned the 1946 Joe Louis Open Championship and title to become the first woman to achieve this honor ever in the history of the Joe Louis Open.

The 1946 United Golfers Association National Open was held in Pittsburgh where Lucy Williams Mitchum won her fourth United Golfers Association National Open Women's Championship. She defeated Hazel Foreman of Washington by 3 and 2.

It is amazing that Lucy Williams had set a record breaking precedent by winning her fourth United Golfers Association National Open title, 1932, 1936, 1937 and 1946. Yet, the media trivialized this moment in history. Only the professional, Pat Ball, preceded her in this feat. Pat Ball won the United Golfers Association Professional Open in 1927, 1929, 1934 and 1941.

Lucy Williams Mitchum entered the 1947 United Golfers Association National Open ready to defend her title and to attempt to win her fifth major title. The tournament was held at the Cobbs Creek Golf Course in Philadelphia. The usual group of women golfers was in contention, including a new group of talented youngsters.

Thelma McTyre Cowans, formerly of Atlanta and now living in Detroit, won her first of five major championship titles. Lucy Williams Mitchum was eliminated from the championship round by Thelma Cowans' sister Theresa Howell, in the quarterfinals.

Some of the other new talent and potential Open winners in the field were Lorraine Sawyer, Hazel Foreman, Mary Brown, Ann Gregory and Eoline Thornton.

The performances of Lucy Williams Mitchum in the United Golfers Association National Opens were coming to an end. She was not in the championship rounds of the 1948, 1949 or 1950 Opens. The Women's Champions were Mary Brown in 1948, Thelma McTyre Cowans in 1949 and Ann Gregory in 1950.

Lucy Williams Mitchum decreased her entries in regional tournaments in 1949 and 1950 and only played in the United Golfers Association majors of 1949 and 1950. Her tournament play reign ended in 1950.

Lucy Williams had made history in the United Golfers Association golf world, but never received the accolades that she was due. She was on par with the amateur and professional men in her accomplishments, but was not given the credit for her abilities. She did not languish in these oversights, but continued to play exceptional golf whenever or wherever she was in a tournament. She was a champion's champion. She was an African American woman champion competing in the world of golf from 1930 to 1950.

Lucy Mitchum & trophies

Lucy Williams Mitchum, (right), with trophies, won from 1927 to 1947.
Photograph courtesy of the Lucy Williams Mitchum Family.

Lucy Mitchum & Dr. Adams

Lucy Williams Mitchum accepts the Joe Louis Women's Championship trophy from Dr. George Adams, UGA president, 1946. Photograph courtesy the Lucy Williams Mitchum Family.

Lucy Mitchum & Joe Louis

Lucy Williams is congratulated by Joe Louis as the first female champion golfer of his tournament, 1946. Photograph courtesy of the Lucy Williams Mitchum Family.

Thelma Cowans - The Rebel

Anyone associated with the United Golfers Association during the 40s and 50s had heard of Thelma McTyre Cowans, the wife of Russ Cowans, the managing editor of the Michigan Chronicle. She is also known as the infamous, and diminutive "bombshell" who broke every rule in the UGA playbook and still walked away with a title. This four time UGA woman champion created such a turmoil, that she was given the 1956 UGA championship title, even after a protest by the women in the tournament.

But, in all fairness to Thelma Cowans, she was a talented golfer who had set her eyes on the ultimate prize in Negro golf – the United Golfers Association National Open Women's Championship. And, with all of the respect that can be given for such an accomplishment, Mrs. Thelma McTyre Cowans was the first woman to win five UGA National Open Women's Championship titles in less than 10 years, 1947 to 1956. And, three of those were in succession. Although, Thelma McTyre Cowans was short in stature, she had a napoleonic winning spirit. She was one of a kind athlete and took no prisoners. She played golf to win the title, to win the trophy, to win the glory and to garner all of the publicity. Even her two sisters, Theresa (Howell) and Dorcas (Riley) were not immune to her attacks on the golf course. They were not given "sisterly" treatment. She beat them like she owned them, then again, the sisters would occasionally win and take a title or two.

Thelma McTyre attended Morris Brown University in Atlanta where she was a multitalented athlete. She was involved in baseball, basketball, soccer, tennis, hockey and track. A physician advised her to take up golf to get into the 'fresh air.' That is when she petitioned the Morris Brown

University Athletic Department to start a golf program. The students played at the Lincoln Golf Course. A golf team was formed and Thelma McTyre was off on a "sports" journey that even she could not have imagined.

Thelma and Theresa McTyre relocated to Detroit and began to play with the Detroit Amateur Golf Club. Playing with the Detroit Club would get them into the tournaments of the United Golfers Association National Open Championships.

Although, Thelma McTyre entered the 1940 UGA Championship, she did not advance to the title flight. However, when Cleo Ball won the 1941 title, Thelma McTyre was in the field to challenge the star power of former champions, like Marie Thompson Jones, Lucy Williams Mitchum and Julia Siler.

She finished in third place to Marie Thompson Jones in the 1941 Amateur Golf Association tournament held at the Riverbank Municipal Golf Course, in Detroit. She was also in the field of the 1942 Midwestern Golf Championship when Lucy Williams Mitchum won the championship title, in Toledo Ohio. Thereafter, she trained to break the elusive championship flight barrier, in order to place among the top entries of the United Golfers National Open Championships.

From 1942 forward, Thelma McTyre was a regular competitor in the local and regional tournaments held in various states when not competing in the United Golfers Association events, such as the -

Avondale Open	Joe Louis Open
Bay Area Open	Midwest Bronze Open
Chicago Women's Golf Club Invitational	Mid-Western Championship
Cosmopolitan Open	Sixth City Open
Desert Mashie Open	Toledo Open
Fairway Open	Vernondale Open

1946 was the year that she became the wife of Russ J. Cowans, the managing editor of the Michigan Chronicle. Russ Cowans was the persona of the weekly columns, "DOWN THE FAIRWAY BY TEE SHOTS" and "RUSS' Corner" by Russ J. Cowans, which appeared as weekly columns in the Chicago Defender.

With all of the good vibes going her way, Thelma McTyre Cowans, broke out of the mix in 1947, as a women's championship trophy winner. Cowans won three tournaments including the 1947 United Golfers Association National Open Women's Championship -

1947 Joe Louis Open	– Philadelphia
1947 Sixth City	– Cleveland
1947 UGA Open	– Philadelphia

The 1947 United Golfers Association National Open Women's Championship was only the beginning of the majors for Thelma Cowans' trail blazing performances. The defending champion was Lucy Williams Mitchum.

The championship flight included Lorraine Sawyer, Hazel Foreman, Amelia Lucas, Roberta Holland, Eloise Sampson, and Clara Reed. It is ironic that Thelma Cowans defeated her sister, Theresa McTyre Howell in the championship round to take the title and the trophy.

The 1948 United Golfers Association National Open was held in Indianapolis and Thelma Mctyre Cowans was the defending champion. Mary Brown won the championship by defeating Thelma Cowans and Hazel Foreman in the semifinal matches. The upset of the tournament was when Ann Gregory was defeated by Hazel Foreman in a semifinal match. Cleo Ball, Sarah Smith and Ann Mahan were also in the championship flight. After giving it her best shot, Thelma Cowans finished second to Mary Brown who won the championship trophy and title by 2 strokes.

The 1949 United Golfers Association National Open Championships were held at the Rackham Golf Course in Detroit. Mary Brown was the defending champion and Thelma Cowans wanted revenge for the lost in 1948.

Again, Thelma Cowans was on familiar turf, her own backyard. This was a perfect setup for a major win.

However, the tournament air was filled with animosity. The diminutive Thelma Cowans was anxious to compete with Mary Brown so that she could take her title back.

Cowans had to focus on taking on Lorraine Sawyer, Hazel Foreman, Sarah Smith, Theresa Howell, the Chicago Women's Club contingent and the other titans that usual found their way into the championship field. But Mary Brown was her primary target. She wanted to prove that she and she alone was the ultimate United Golfers Association Open Women's Champion.

The reporter's description was that Mrs. Cowans "played the best golf of her career" to capture the 1949 title and her second major win. However, the win was really minimized because Mary Brown, her nemesis, was the second place finisher.

After the tournament, in the Fall of 1949, Thelma Cowans relocated to Los Angeles California. She became a member of the Vernondale Golf Club formed by Mae Crowder. Her sister, Dorcas Riley and Maggie Hathaway were also members of the Vernondale Golf Club.

From 1950 to 1953, Cowans contended in each of the United Golfers Association Open Championships. She continued to train mentally and physically to concentrate on the UGA Open Championships.

The 1950 United Golfers Association was held in Washington. Thelma Cowans was the defending champion. Ann Gregory won the 1950 championship and Thelma Cowans finished in third place.

In 1951, Thelma Cowans was in the field, but did not advance to the championship round. However, 1951 was to be the year for Eoline Thornton of Los Angeles to capture the United Golfers Association National Open Women's title and trophy.

Pittsburgh was the site of the 1952 United Golfers Association Open. Eoline Thornton, the defending champion was ousted by Alice Stewart of Detroit.

Fireworks were exhibited in the 1953 United Golfers Association Championships. The site was Kansas City. Thelma Cowans made a charge to win, but suffered a setback in the semifinals and finished in fourth place. Theresa Howell, her sister finished in second place to the 1953 champion – Ann Gregory.

With the resolve of a committed champion, Thelma Cowans vowed to engrave her name into the annals of the history of the United Golfers Association. She began at the 1954 Open Championships held in Dallas Texas. Ann Gregory could not defend the 1953 title because of a sprained ankle. This was the jump start that Cowans needed.

The field was deep with most of the former champions and second place finishers. However, to win this unprecedented event, Thelma Cowans had to defeat one of her nemeses, Eoline Thornton, also of Los Angeles, to win her third major victory - the 1954 title and trophy. Cowans was barely able to win over Eoline Thornton by 1 up on the 19th hole. Cowans was down in the first seven holes, but was able to recover by the 18th hole. The victory was sweet as she held up her 3rd UGA National Open Women Championship trophy.

In 1955, the United Golfers Association was held in Detroit. Thelma Cowans was delighted to show off her skills in front of the old hometown crowd. She was back with the fire of a three time champion golfer. She was in good form as she defeated Lorraine Sawyer, Frances Mays, Juanita Goodson, Myrtle McIver, Ann Gregory and her sister, Theresa Howell to enter into the winner's circle. This was the second time that Cowans had to defeat Lorraine Sawyer for the championship title. Thelma Cowans had just won her fourth major United Golfers Association National Open Women's titles and the trophy.

The 1956 United Golfers Association National Open Championships started on time at 6:00AM. Every golfer was in position at the Cobbs Creek Golf Course in Philadelphia. Everyone was in place except Thelma Cowans. Her playing competitor, in the final championship round, was Alma Arvin of Baltimore. The results of that day were the most negative in the career of a great champion. Thelma Cowans did not display good judgment or sportsmanship, when she finally arrived. The Rules Committee contributed to the fiasco by not adhering to the rules and awarded the championship title to Thelma Cowans. The 1956 championship title was her third consecutive championship title and her fifth overall major United Golfers Association National Open Women's Champion title and trophy.

Thelma Cowans had realized her goals, to be the best and to be the first. She was the first woman to win the United Golfers Association Women's Championship five times. She had stamped her name in the history of the United Golfers Association.

After the 1956 fiasco, Thelma Cowans retreated to the West Coast and began a new life. She had done what she had to in order to fulfill a dream of being the best among the most talented United Golfers Association women players.

Thelma McTyre Cowans was a formidable golf opponent. Her golf feats are surpassed only by Ann Gregory, Ethel Funches and Lucy Williams Mitchum as one of the most competitive women on the United Golfers Association circuit. Cowans won the National Women's Open four times and was given the title in 1956 –

1947 in Philadelphia, PA
1949 in Detroit, MI
1954 in Dallas TX
1955 in Detroit, MI
[1956 in Philadelphia, PA]

Thelma Cowans was elected to the National Afro-American Golfers Hall of Fame in 1971.

N.B.

It is unfortunate that the newspaper photographs of Thelma McTyre Cowans are over 60 years old and do not have the clarity required to be reproduced in this volume. For the ones interested in viewing photographs of the diminutive dynamo of the United Golfers Association National Open Women's Champions you can access the following photographs of Thelma McTyre Cowans in the microfilm format of the Chicago Defender –

1. Thelma Cowans is presented the 1949 UGA Women's Championship trophy by the Governor of Michigan, G. Mennen Williams. Chicago Defender, September 3, 1949, 15.
2. Thelma Cowans Plotting Victorious Swing East…by A. S. Doc Young. Photographs of her tropies, swing and putting. Chicago Defender, May 20, 1950, 18.
3. Thelma Cowans is presented her third UGA National Open Women's trophy, 1954. Chicago Defender, September 11, 1954, 10.

1966 CLUB CHAMPIONS

Thelma Cowans & champions

Left to right: William Barnes, Frankie Wyche, Earnest Parish. Thelma Cowans and Charles Dryer. Photograph courtesy of Exie Shackelford-Ochier.

Ann Moore Gregory
The Queen of Negro Golf

Ann Moore Gregory was a pioneer in the truest sense of the word. She was a trailblazer on the frontiers of athletics, social justice and civil rights, including establishing a presence as an United States Golf Association Amateur golf pioneer.

Ann Moore was born to Henry and Myra Moore in Aberdeen, Mississippi. She was the middle child of five children. Following the death of her parents, she worked as a live-in maid of a white family in Aberdeen, while she was still a teenager. The family, to its credit made sure that Ann finished high school. Upon graduating from high school, in 1930, Ann headed to Gary, Indiana to live with an older sister.

Being a natural athlete, she began to play tennis. By 1937, she had displayed such tremendous talent that she won the Gary City Championship in the same year. Her athletic prowess led her to associate with other avid sports participants. During these social gatherings, she met Leroy Percy Gregory, an employee of U. S. Steel. "Percy" was an avid golfer who played whenever he had the opportunity and eventually introduced Ann to the sport.

Percy and Ann were married in 1938. And, soon the two became a family of three with the birth of their only child, JoAnn in 1942. By 1943, World War II intervened and Percy was drafted into the Navy. Although the game of golf had been a source of some contention early in their marriage, Ann began to play golf to pass the lonely hours while her husband was away during the war. By the time he was honorably discharged from the service and returned home, Ann had developed a propensity for the game. Her golf coach was Calvin Ingraham, a notable golfer in the Chicago area.

By serendipity, Ann Gregory was observed playing on a course at the same time as a group of women from the Chicago Women's Golf Club were playing. She was soon invited to become a member and joined the Chicago Women's Golf Club in 1945. She also entered her first Chicago Women's Golf Club Midwest tournament in July 1945 and finished second to Myrtle Ford. In 1948, she won her first tournament, sponsored by the Sunset Hills Country Club in St Anne, Illinois. Lucy Williams (Mitchum) finished second, Cleo Ball was third and Geneva Wilson finished in fourth place. Mrs. Gregory also finished fourth in the 1948 United Golfers Association National Open Women's Championship.

By this time, Ann Gregory was balancing a full plate of responsibilities. She maintained a household in Gary, Indiana, was raising a daughter, worked as a caterer, did volunteer work obtaining funds for the Community Chest and United Fund, as well as serving on the Board of Directors of the Gary Public Library. Somehow, she was able to fit the commute to Chicago within an hour to participate with the Chicago Women's Golf Club.

Ann had a commute of 32 miles from Gary, Indiana to Chicago, Illinois, but Ann rarely missed a meeting or a tournament. The Chicago Women's Golf Club was formed on November 16, 1937 by Anna Mae Black (Robinson), Vivian Pitts and Cleo Ball.

The Chicago Women's Golf Club presidents during the Ann Gregory golf reign were –

1937/39 Anna Black	1952/53 Mary Campbell
1940/42 Dorothy Hooks	1954/55 Geraldine Williams
1943/44 Fettia Bellinger	1956/57 Lydia Adams
1945/46 Ella Morphis	1958/58 Joylyn Robicheaux
1947/48 Blanche Bowman	1959/59 Maxine Harris
1949/50 Hattie Davenport	1960/60 Anna Black Robinson
1951/52 Bernice Kelly	

The leadership ability of the presidents during the innovative period of 1937 to 1960 gave Ann Gregory the opportunity to become the "Queen of Negro Golf."

During a span of 50 years, Ann Gregory won at least 25 Chicago Women's Golf Club titled events, in addition to her other golf victories nationwide. There was a cadre of women who competitively pressed Ann Gregory for a title. The women were frequently in many of the championship flights vying for a title - Hazel Bibbs, Thelma Cowans, Theresa Howell, Alice Stewart and Eoline Thornton.

A partial list of the local and regional tournament wins of Ann Gregory as a member of the Chicago Women's Golf Club (1945-1980):

Charles F. Armstrong Memorial	Minnesota Open
Chicago Women's Golf Club Annual	Pepsi-Cola International
Chicago Women's Golf Club Classic	Pitch & Putt (Detroit)
Chicago Women's Golf Club Championship	Sixth City (Cleveland OH)
Chicago Women's Golf Club Invitational	Sunset Hills Club
CWGC Midwest/Walter Speedy Memorial	Joe Louis Invitational
Fairway Golf (Dayton OH)	Vehicle City Open
Flint Open (Flint MI)	Windy City (Chicago IL)

Ann Gregory entered into many of the UGA National Open Women's Championships and is among a group of elite women who have won five of the prestigious titles. Mrs. Gregory won the title in 1950, 1953, 1957 and back to back in 1965 and 1966. Ann Gregory's first experience in the championship round of the UGA National Open was in 1948. She finished second to the 1948 Women's champion, Mary Brown. The 1949 UGA National Open was also a year of champion drought.

The 1950 Championship was held in Washington DC and consisted of a field of 35 women. Thelma Cowans was the defending champion and Mary Brown was a contender. Eoline Thornton defeated Thelma Cowans, in the semifinals to participate in the final round. Ann Gregory, "the housewife from Gary, Indiana" defeated Eoline Thornton of Los Angeles with a score of 4 and 3 to win the championship title.

Ann Gregory was unable to defend the championship title in 1951. Eoline Thornton of Los Angeles claimed the title of United Golfers National Open Women's Champion. In 1952, Ann Gregory was in the final championship group, but finished second to Alice Stewart of Detroit in competition for the title.

The 1953 United Golfers Association National Open was held in Kansas City where Ann Gregory won her second Championship title. The defending champion was Alice Stewart of Detroit. The championship flight included Alice Stewart, Theresa Howell, Lorraine Sawyer and Thelma Cowans. Theresa Howell defeated Lorraine Sawyer and Alice Stewart to get into the final match for the championship. Ann Gregory eventually defeated Thelma Cowans and Theresa Howell for the 1953 UGA title.

Ann Gregory withdrew from the 1954 UGA National Open Championship because of a sprained ankle she incurred a week prior to the event. Thelma Cowans won the title by defeating Eoline Thonrton.

Mrs. Gregory added three more United Golfers Association National Open Champonship titles to her growing list of accomplishments. She won in 1957 in Washington DC, the site of her first title. Her last United Golfers Association titles were won in succession in 1965 at Detroit and at Chicago in 1966.

The Chicago Women's Golf Club joined the United States Golf Association to give Ann Gregory the opportunity to play in the USGA Women's Amateur Championship. In 1956, Ann Gregory stood on the first tee at the Meridian Hills County Club in Indianapolis on September 17, 1956.

She did not win the USGA trophy, but, she had won the ultimate prize of integrating the playing field of the Women's Amateur golf tournament. On that day, all of America knew that Mrs. Ann Moore Gregory of Gary Indiana had arrived.

Ann Gregory continued to play in most of the USGA tournaments until 1988/1989. She had stepped into a new world fraught with competitive jealousy and blatant racism. She was no longer the 'Queen of Negro Golf'. Her African American compatriots were making derisive comments and the Caucasians were casting negative dispersions. However, this did not deter her. Ann Gregory took it all in and weighed the pros and cons of her decision.

During this period of her life, Ann Gregory became a talented, patient and leading civil rights athlete within the golf community. She smiled and quelled the critics. She busted drives and quelled the critics. She one putted and quelled the critics. She went about the business of playing golf as an athlete and quelled the critics.

Ann Gregory became the Ambassador of "accept me as I am and you will believe." Not only did they believe, but everyone fell in love and showed respect for Mrs. Ann Moore Gregory, the woman, the athlete, the golfer.

Gregory had reduced her playing activities in the UGA tournament, during the sixties, to participate in more United States Golf Association events.

1966 Hall of Fame inductees

1966 UGA Hall of Fame Inductees: Ann Gregory, Maxwell Stanford and Mary Campbell. Photograph courtesy of Exie Shackelford-Ochier.

Ann Gregory USGA Tournament Record

USGA - Women's Open

Year	Course	Finish	Score	To Par
1956	Northland CC, MN	WD	85-94-93=272	+49
1963	Kenwood CC, OH	CUT	86-83=160	+23
1966	Hazeltine National GC,MN	CUT	93-84=177	+33
1968	Moselem Springs GC, Pa	CUT	87-86=173	+31
1972	Winged Foot Golf Club, NY	CUT	91-87=178	+34

USGA - Women's Amateur

Year	Course	Finish	Score
1956	Meridian Hills Country Club, IN	T-65	Match Play Results (Round 1 lost to Mrs. Philip Cudone)
1959	Congressional Country Club, DC	T-17	Match Play Results (Round 3 lost to Diana Hoke)
1960	Tulsa Country Club, OK	T-33	Match Play Results (Round 2 lost to Kathleen Newton)
1962	Country Club of Rochester, NY	T-65	Match Play Results (Round 1 lost to Mrs. Joseph Nesbitt)
1963	Taconic Golf Club, MA	T-65	Match Play Results (Round 1 lost to Carol Sorenson)

USGA - Senior Women's Amateur

Year	Course	Finish	Score
1971	Sea Island Golf Club, GA	2	77-82-78=237
1972	Manufacturers Golf & Country Club, PA	T-5	80-86-83=249
1974	Lakewood Golf Club, AL	T-15	87-85-83=255
1975	Rhode Island Country Club, RI	35	88-94-92=274

1976	Monterey Peninsula Country Club, CA	T-8	83-84-85=252
1977	Dunes Golf & Beach Club, SC	16	81-85-84=250
1978	Rancho Bernardo Golf Club, CA	T-51	85-89-85=259
1979	Hardscrabble Country Club, AR	T-18	81-88-79=248
1980	Sea Island Golf Club, GA	T-6	84-81-80=245
1981	Spring Lake Golf Club, NJ	T-18	86-86-86=258
1982	Kissing Camels Golf Club, CO	T-58	90-92-91=273
1983	Gulph Mills Golf Club, PA	T-49	94-95-85=274
1984	Tacoma Country & Golf Club, WA	T-52	94-89-79=262
1988	Sea Island Golf Club, GA	T-85	88-88-92=268
1989	Tournament Players Course, TX	T-65	94-89-93=276

Tournament records reproduced with the permission of the Museum & Archives Register, U.S.G.A., Far Hills NJ.

In a career that spanned five decades, Ann Gregory won over three hundred tournaments. Her most crowning achievement came in 1989, while mourning the death of her husband of fifty years, and at the age of 76. She beat anyone over the age of 50 to win the Gold medal in the U.S. Senior Olympics.

Ann Gregory is honored for her achievements by two African American Golf Halls of Fame – the National Afro-American Golfers Hall of Fame in 1966 and the African American Golfers Hall of Fame in 2006.

Her athletic prowess and grace under pressure was written in an article by Rhonda Glenn entitled, *Playing Through Racial Barriers*. The closing paragraph states, "She teed it up during a difficult era, against odds that few of us can ever know. She endured painful slights with warmth, humor, courage, and good sense. More than most of us, she cherished the game, and in the end, she honored it. I knew Ann Gregory. She was simply a golfer, a very fine one."

To honor her memory, the Urban Chamber of Commerce of Las Vegas annually hosts a tournament in her name – The Annual Ann Gregory Memorial Scholarship Golf Tournament in August.

The persona of Ann Gregory was to glide over the negative and embellish the positive. She did what she was destined to do – to have the future generations of women golfers to review her accomplishments, then to take their talents to the next level of greatness without fear.

Ethel Powers Funches
The Ultimate African American Woman Golfer

Ethel Funches was born in the South when "Blackness" was a negative. But, she was not to be deterred. When Ethel arrived in Washington DC, she was a survivor and ready for any challenge. Eugene Funches taught his wife, Ethel how to play golf so that she could join the prestigious Wake Robin Golf Club. If she could play golf then she would have some women to socialize with during the week. Eugene Funches did not know that he was unleashing the most phenomenal woman athlete in the history of African American golf.

Ethel Funches was born ahead of her time. She should have been born during the era of the "First Tee" program. She was a natural born athlete with the inner spirit and strength of a winner. She would have been identified as a "Phenom" according to the standards of today for a woman who learned how to play golf as an adult. She probably would have blown the LPGA wide open with amazement.

Ethel Funches was finally invited to join the Wake Robin Golf Club in 1943. The Wake Robin Golf Club represented the crème de la crème of Washington society. That did not bother Ethel Funches because she was to use the club as a conduit to become part of golf history. She had the nerve and the talent to challenge the status quo of the elite Wake Robin Club Championship hierarchy.

Although, Ethel Funches had an exterior calm and friendly demeanor, she was the fiercest golf competitor that the Wake Robin members had ever encountered. She was always smiling as she set her sights on taking a hole or an entire tournament away from an opponent. She played the game to win and to win only. It took nine years for her to become the number one Wake

Robin Golf Club Champion. Then when she was ready and had analyzed the games of the Club Champions, Ethel Funches stepped forward to make her bid for the Championship title. She had to displace Sarah Smith, Ethel Terrell, Elizabeth Rice, Hazel Foreman and Frances Mays as the multiple champion title holders. She became the dominating force to be reckoned with in the Wake Robin Golf Club Championships. Ethel Funches won 14 of the 27 Club Championships between 1952 and 1978.

Wake Robin Golf Club Champions, 1937-1980

1937 Sarah Smith	1959 Ethel Funches
1938 Sarah Smith	1960 Elizabeth Rice
1939 Ethel Terrell	1961 Ethel Funches
1940 Sarah Smith	1962 Ethel Funches
1941 Ethel Terrell	1963 Alma Arvin
1942 Hazel Foreman	1964 Ethel Funches
1943 Ethel Terrell	1965 Elizabeth Rice
1944 Magnolia Reynolds	1966 Frances Mays
1945 Sarah Smith	1967 Frances Mays
1946 Hazel Foreman	1968 Alma Arvin
1947 Magnolia Reynolds	1969 Ethel Funches
1948 Hazel Foreman	1970 Vernice Logan
1949 Elizabeth Rice	1971 Ethel Funches
1950 Amelia Lucas	1972 Laurie Stokien
1951 Elizabeth Rice	1973 Ethel Funches
1952 Ethel Funches	1974 Laurie Stokien
1953 Ethel Funches	1975 Laurie Stokien
1954 Ethel Funches	1976 Laurie Stokien
1955 Ethel Funches	1977 Frances Mays
1956 Elizabeth Rice	1978 Ethel Funches
1957 Ethel Funches	1979 Elizabeth Rice
1958 Ethel Funches	1980 Frances Mays

It appeared as if Ethel Funches was honing her skills to explore other golf horizons. She began to participate in various regional tournaments held up and down the East Coast with her husband, Eugene, as her caddy.

She captured multiple championship trophies and titles in events such as the –

D.C. Recreation Open	New Jersey State Open
Eastern Golf Association Open	Maryland State Open
Pennsylvania State Open	Green's Ladies Annual
Howard University "H" Club Tourney	Ballentine's 3-Ring Golf Classic

Rheingold's Tournament of Champions

The trophies were accumulating so fast that the Funches' had to allocate a separate room to display the most prestigious ones. Ethel Funches had not only become the darling of the Wake Robin Golf Club, but she had captured the devotion of the entire East Coast. She was designated as the one to break the Midwestern hold on the United Golfers Association National Open Women's Championship.

The Open Championships were held at various golf venues throughout the United States. This meant that Ethel Funches had to compete against the most dominate women players since 1946. Lucy Williams Mitchum, Thelma McTyre Cowans, Ann Gregory, Vernice Turner, Eoline Thornton, Geneva Wilson, Mary Brown and the sisterhood of the Chicago Women's Golf Club were waiting to dispose of the East Coast rookie.

By 1955, Ethel Funches was ready to accept the challenge of the Queens of the United Golfers Association National Open Women's Championship. The Opens were held in Detroit. Thelma Cowans defeated Ethel Funches and won her fourth Championship title. Although it did not bode well with Funches, at least she finished in second place.

The 1956 Open Championships were held in Philadelphia where Thelma Cowans was the cause of an unfortunate incident. Many of the women golfers were disappointed with the outcome, but Thelma McTyre Cowans was handed her fifth Championship title.

1957 was another year to make things happen on the United Golfers Association National Open Championships. The site of the tournaments was in the Washington DC area. Ethel Funches would be on familiar territory and had a chance to take the trophy and the title. Unfortunately, this was also the site of Ann Gregory's first win in 1950. Ann Gregory won her third Open Women's title and Ethel Funches finished in second place.

It is a good thing that Eugene Funches was his wife's caddy because he was able to keep her focused on the task at hand. Just play to win, everything else will fall in place. So, when the 1958 National Open Championships rolled around, Ethel Funches was ready. This time the Opens were held in Pittsburgh. The outcome of the women's tournament brought tears of joy and tears of disappointment to Ethel and Eugene Funches. Ethel's close friend, Vernice Turner had won the championship and had put Ethel's hopes again on the back burner.

It was Vernice Turner who motivated Ethel Funches to go for the 1959 Open Championship title because it was being held in Washington DC again. Vernice Turner and Elizabeth Rice pushed Ethel Funches to the final segment of the Championship round. Ethel Funches finally made her debut as the 1959 United Golfers Association National Open Women's Champion.

In 1960, Ethel Funches set out to prove that she was not a one time accidental Open Champion. The 1960 site for the Open Championships was Chicago at the Rackham and Pipe O' Peace Golf Clubs. The Midwestern contingent was geared up to dethrone the neophyte. Ethel Funches with Eugene Funches by her side defended her Championship trophy and the title. Ethel Funches had won the United Golfers Association National Open Women's Championship two years in a row, 1959 and 1960.

In 1961, Ethel Funches was geared up to add another United Golfers Association National Open Women's Championship to her collection. The Open Championships were to be held in Boston MA. This East Coast site was suited for her game. However, as fate would have it, she was bested again by her close friend, Vernice Turner. And, then in 1962, she was ousted by an unknown, Carrie Jones.

Ethel Funches was playing good golf, but had made some slight mistakes that prevented her from taking the former two titles. So, the Funches' had to regroup and focus on not when to win, but, how to win the United Golfers Association National Open major. This time the Open was held again in Washington DC. There were no excuses to be made. She had done it before and now it was time to go for her third Open Championship. Now was the time to meet the challenge of Lucy Williams Mitchum and Thelma McTyre Cowans and Ann Gregory. It was not easy, but Ethel Funches prevailed and won her third United Golfers Association National Open Women's Championship trophy and title in the year, 1963.

It appeared as if Ethel Funches had hit her peak. The years, 1964, 1965 and 1966 rolled by without a United Golfers Association National Open major win. During the negative publicity about the major, many forgot that Ethel Funches was still in contention and winning in local and regional tournaments. Perhaps this is what stirred up the fire in her during the Open Championships in 1967, 1968, 1969 and 1973.

Ethel Funches with her husband Eugene, as her caddy eclipsed all of the United Golfers Association National Open Championships - Men's Amateur, Men's Professional and Women's Amateur win records.

In a short span of time, Ethel Funches won over 100 local and regional titles and trophies. She reached her goal of becoming the best woman African American amateur golfer in the nation.

Ethel Funches who dissected the Wake Robin Club Champions and became the Women's Champion of Champions, took on the United Golfers Association to become the most dynamic National Open Women's Champion in history.

Ethel P. Funches was inducted into the Afro-American Golfers Hall of Fame in 1970.

Ethel Powers Funches
United Golfers Association National Open Women's Champion
1914 – January 06, 2010

Ethel Funches & trophy

Ethel Funches with "Championship" trophy presented by J. F. Cook, GM of Ballentine & Sons, 1956. Photograph credit: The PUTTER Magazine.

I am an African American Woman Golfer
I established the first Golf Club to play
I proved that I could compete and win
I did it and so can you
Be a Champion

PART TWO

Changing the Scene

1. A Rare Pair

Vernice Turner and Madelyn Turner

A MOTHER AND HER CADDY

There is no way to describe the bond between a mother and her daughter. The love that flows from one to the other can be the most positive relationship between two human beings. On the other hand it can reek of frustrations when the daughter begins to grow up or when the two are in competition with each other for honor and glory.

The bonding between Vernice Turner and her daughter, Madelyn, was an exception. They both learned how to play golf together. They practiced together to tune up for the local and regional tournaments. They were taught the game and supported by the hero of the family, David Turner.

One day it came to past that the mom, Vernice Turner, needed a caddy who knew her game and could keep her focused on the task – to win a title and a trophy. The most obvious and logical choice was Madelyn Turner, her daughter. The mother and daughter caddy duo has never been duplicated in the history of golf during the UGA tour or the current LPGA tour. They were and always will be in a class by themselves.

This is their story.

Vernice Turner
Two Time United Golfers
Association Champion

I live in a small town on the seashore of New Jersey. The name of the town is Ocean City and is located a 'hop and skip' from the gambling capital of the East Coast - Atlantic City NJ.

My family played golf out of the Apex Golf Club of Pomona NJ. My family consisted of David Sr., Janet, Madelyn and David Jr. David Sr. was the recreational guru of the family and made sure that the family was involved in many sports activities on the weekends. So, during the winter it was bowling and during the summer it was golf. David Sr. was the instructor and coach for the family. I was the wife, mother, chauffer, cheerleader and first–aid administrator. Dave Sr. was always attempting to keep his children busy so that they would not get into trouble. However, during the process and sessions, I began to pick up the intricacies of the games while watching over the three children.

The watching and practicing developed into the thought of trying the game of golf for real. I wanted to find out if I could compete with the women of the Apex Club. I began to sharpen the skills on the weekends and finally summoned up the courage to enter into an Apex Club event. The membership and I were surprised when I won a trophy. This victory gave me the incentive to enter into more local tournaments and some of the regional tournaments. My favorite regional events were the ones sponsored by the Green's Ladies of Philadelphia. It was at one of their tournaments that I met Ethel Funches of the Wake Robin Golf Club located in Washington. Ethel Funches and I developed a close friendship as well as a positive golf game rivalry

Soon, I began to branch out to play in the following tournaments where I was challenged by the best of the best women amateur golfers.

Pennsylvania Open	New York Open	New Jersey Open
Cape Cod Capesters	Springfield MA Open	Quaker City Open
Mid-Western Open	Chicago Women's Golf Club Tournaments	
Wake Robin Golf Club Annuals	Green's Ladies Tournaments	

After reviewing my performances, there was no question as to if I could make it to the United Golfers Association National Open Championships. The goal of the family was for me, the Ocean City NJ mom, to win a United Golfers Association National Open Women's Championship.

Beginning in 1955, I had put myself in the position to win the title several times. However, I would always fade away in the Championship round when paired with a long hitter. I was short off of the tee, but accurate from the fairway to the green.

In 1956 the United Golfers Association National Open Championships were held in Pittsburgh where Thelma Cowans was awarded the title. The 1957 Open Championships were held in Washington with Ann Gregory as the title holder.

The 1958 United Golfers Association National Open Amateur Women's Championship was held in Pittsburgh. I was familiar with the site and my close friend Ethel Funches was in the Championship flight. I played the best golf of my life to overtake Myrtle Patterson, Elizabeth Rice, Alma Arvin, Teresa Tabron, Eoline Thornton, and finally, Ethel Funches.

My husband and three children were witness to me, the Ocean City, NJ housewife and mom, as the winner of the 1958 United Golfers Association National Open Women's Amateur title. Finally, Ocean City, NJ had a star athlete in its midst. And this accomplishment by a local citizen put Ocean City on the map along with Atlantic City.

In 1959 and 1960, I was overshadowed by my golf buddy, Ethel Funches who won the two titles. But, I was not to be deterred and was encouraged by Ethel Funches and others to focus on the 1961 title. 1961 was a year where I had to focus on the children. Janet and Madelyn were in their teens and David Jr. was nine. This was no time for a mom to be chasing after a golf title. However, with the blessing of the family, I gave it one more attempt at a title. My family and I traveled to Boston to enter into the 1961 United Golfers Association National Open Championships.

The 1961 United Golfers Association National Open Championships were held at the Ponkapaog Golf Course outside of Boston MA. The whole Turner Family was there. David Turner Sr. was competing in the Men's Amateur Division, I was competing in the Women's Amateur Division and Madelyn was competing in the Amateur Junior Girls Division.

Madelyn Turner had won the Girl's Junior Title earlier in the week, which gave me the incentive to try to win the major title. Madelyn was ready to caddy for the victory.

My close friend, Ethel Funches and I had made it to the final Championship round. I was barely able to eke out a win of 2 and 1 in match play over Ethel Funches. In the meantime, David Turner Sr. did not fair too well at the tournament. He was eliminated early. But, that did not bother him because his wife and daughter had won the major amateur trophies of the 1961 United Golfers Association National Open Championships.

This was the first mother and daughter title wins as individual players and the first mother daughter-caddy team in the history of the Open Championships. We were and still are "one of a kind."

The family celebrated, the Apex Club celebrated and Ocean City celebrated because not only did we win, but we were a repeat. When we all settled down, we began to concentrate on a sport that would keep the family close to home – bowling. Since 1961, I have won many bowling titles and trophies.

As an author, I regret that I was not able to give Mrs. Vernice Turner a personal copy of this book. She invited me into her home with open arms and took me on a historic tour of African American golf. THANK YOU.

Vernice Harris Turner
April 3, 1923 – August 17, 2009

VERNICE HARRIS TURNER

Vernice Turner

Vernice Turner, winner of the 1958 and 1961 UGA National Open Women's Championships. Photograph courtesy of the David and Vernice Turner Family.

Madelyn "Moochie" Turner
Mom's Caddy

I began to play golf at the age of ten years old. I was not coached formally by a golf professional. My father, David Turner developed my talents and expertise to play the game. My dad was an avid golfer and began teaching me and my mom the essentials and mechanisms inherent to the development of a good golf game. My parents took me with them every time they went to a golf course. It appeared as if I was always in a golf paradise.

The Apex Golf Course in Pomona, New Jersey was our home course. I represented Apex as a junior golfer in the United Golfers Association and the Eastern Golf Association. We traveled from Ocean City NJ to Boston MA to Washington DC to Chicago IL to compete in golf tournaments. I was really competitive and wanted to win all of the time. Some of the girls on the Junior Golf circuit were Jean Robertson of Chicago, Renee Powell of East Canton, Juanita Arvin of Baltimore and Deborah Rhodes of St Louis. There were many more of them vying for the coveted United Golfers Association National Open Junior Girls Championship.

I was in an elite group of junior girl golfers who won United Golfers Association National Open Junior Championship trophies –

1959 UGA National Open Junior Girls Championship, 9-14 years old, Washington DC
1960 UGA National Open Junior Girls Championship, under 14 years old, Chicago IL
1961 UGA National Open Junior Girls Championship, Boston MA

Some other first place finishes include –

> 1961 Quaker City Golf Club tournament
> 1961 Radio Station "WHAT"-NAACP tournament
> 1961 TIOGA golf tournament

Most of the time, I was the caddy for my mother in her bids for the United Golfers Association Women's Championships. My dad had taught me well as to how to handle and support a golfer in a competitive situation. A golfer and the caddy have to form a united bond to see shots and to execute shots to get the ball in the hole. My mom and I were exceptional as a team because we thought alike. We were one unit out on the golf course. We were the first and only mother and daughter golf team on the United Golfers Association Tour. It made me so proud to be known as mom's caddy or "Little Turner."

Being mom's caddy during her tournaments gave me the opportunity to meet some celebrity and championship golfers such as Ann Gregory, Ethel Funches, Renee Powell, Althea Gibson, Joe Louis, Harry Wheeler, Charlie Sifford, Lee Elder and many others too numerous to name individually. However, there was one person, in particular that I do remember, a Mr. Chick Stewart of Baltimore MD. Mr. Stewart always teased me about throwing golf clubs and cursing at my young age. In his own way, he was trying to teach me the etiquette of the game of golf, always be a lady, win or lose.

One of my great memories was when I caddied for my mother and she was playing in a threesome with Ethel Funches and Althea Gibson. I always loved when my mother and Ethel Funches played together. They were opponents, yet, the best of friends. They had the respect for each other's golf game and taught me a lot about the nuances inherent in the rules in the game of golf as a sport, and friendship.

When I was in high school and college, there were no formal golf teams. So, playing golf was a weekend family activity. I was not privy to the athletic golf scholarships when I was ready to enter college. Even the United Golfers Association did not offer scholarships for girls to continue to play in the colleges or to choose golf as a career. So, I did not play competitive golf in college. As a result, I lost all interest in the sport. Nor, when I was actively employed, did I participate in playing golf socially at any point.

My mom, Vernice Turner won the United Golfers Association National Open Women's Championship two times, 1958 and 1961. The most significant achievement in our historical mother / daughter relationship was in 1961. I won the National Open Junior Girls Championship and she won the National Open Women's Championship during the same tournament week. We have been the only mother / daughter National Open Champions in the history of the United Golfers Association.

As I reflect back to that moment, I do wish that we had preserved our score cards as part of golf history.

When I retired from working at the Federal Bureau of Investigation, my co-workers and friends gave me a set of NIKE slingshot clubs. This gesture gave me the incentive to become involved in the sport of golf again. I have started to play and now work, part time, at the Forest Green Golf Course in Quantico Virginia.

Madelyn Turner

Madelyn Turner with the 1959, 1960 and 1961 United Golfers Association National Open Junior Girls Championship trophies. Photograph courtesy of Madelyn Turner.

2. The Revolutionists
Maggie Hathaway
Althea Gibson

A REVOLUTIONIST

A revolutionist is one who advocates radical changes in the racial, political or cultural segments in a status quo society. Maggie Hathaway and Althea Gibson were definitely proponents of advocating societal change.

Maggie Hathaway and Althea Gibson were like the East Coast versus the West Coast in their approach to the racial equality of the African American as a citizen of these United States of America.

Maggie Hathaway was very vocal and animated about what should be done and how it should be done to produce equality in the work place and society. Maggie Hathaway played the race card whenever it was conducive to do so. That is how she was able to make the movie industry change many of their hiring and wage policies. This was the weapon she used to make the sport of golf more available to minorities.

Althea Gibson took the affirmative approach that your talents should represent you in any arena, regardless of the race card. Althea Gibson was a warrior in an athletic way. She would indicate to her foes – "here I am to participate in a sports event, you have to resolve the situation the best that you can."

They both achieved their ultimate goals for bringing change to the racial climate in America.

Maggie Hathaway - The Civil Rights Leader

Maggie Hathaway, of Shreveport LA, was born to chart her own destiny. As a teenager, she left her family and headed for Hollywood to reap her fame and fortune, during the 1930's. She had anticipated that her Louisiana beauty queen features would dazzle the movie moguls to promote her as a screen star.

Hathaway bounced from one small role to the other without ever realizing her dream of becoming a star in the film industry. During her ordeals, she was made painfully aware of the unfair employment practices that existed in the industry.

She began to organize the minorities into groups to demonstrate and voice their dissatisfaction with the negative treatment and low paying job offers. The first protest march and boycott of the movie industry was in 1946. As a result, the industry began to make some extraordinary changes to improve upon the declining race relations.

She was identified as a labor activist and known to be a troublemaker wherever she went. She had found her calling as a civil rights leader. She finally achieved stardom in the movie industry as the female change agent.

By 1954, the industry and Maggie Hathaway parted ways. She developed an affinity for golf and was a member of the Vernondale Golf Club for Women. The first golf protest she led was against the Western Avenue Women's Golf Club because they had rejected her membership application. Although the Western Avenue Women's Club eventually admitted minorities, the feud between the two parties lasted for years.

It was to be several decades, before Maggie Hathaway would be invited to join the Club. She accepted the invitation and then immediately resigned from the membership. It was too late to attempt to appease Maggie Hathaway.

Maggie Hathaway also began to protest the denial of minorities to have access to public golf courses within the county. Her protest was that "all people should be able to use any public recreational facility, since the government uses the taxpayer's money for the maintenance of the parks and golf courses." The marches and protests ignited an everlasting symbiotic pact between Hathaway and the County Supervisor, Kenneth Hahn. She would continue the protests on the outside while he would work within the system to renovate it to make the governance equal for all people.

During this period of time, she was responsible for establishing the Minority Association for Golfers (MAG). The purpose of the organization was to empower all people interested in the sport of golf. The group would collectively protect the minorities who applied for any job that was associated with the sport of golf. The employment would range from caddy to greens keeper to pro shop managers to club house staff.

By 1962, Maggie Hathaway had established the Beverly Hills chapter of the National Association for the Advancement of Colored People (NAACP). It was through her social encounters with some of the stars of the entertainment business that she was able to establish the "Image Awards." The Awards were to acknowledge the accomplishments of African Americans in the film industry.

Maggie Hathaway also championed for the African American male golfers, such as Charlie Sifford and Lee Elder to obtain the privileges to play on pristine golf courses so that they could compete on the PGA tour.

Maggie Hathaway was labeled as a trouble maker, a rebel, an activist and a divisive character. But, Maggie Hathaway was ahead of her time. She had witnessed the racial inequities and tried to make them right. As a woman, she was often alone, but she kept trying until someone heard her voice and realized what she was trying to do.

Maggie Hathaway was a social activist. She grew up in a segregated environment of the South. She ran away from it to establish a new life in the state of California. She was disappointed when she was slapped in the face with racism in pursuit of her acting career. She finally became a visionary as to race relations and decided to devote her life to making a change.

She was the civil rights protester, she was the picket line organizer, she was the rebel rouser, she was the 'mover and shaker' in racial turmoil.

Her territory was basically in California, but her message was heard all over the world.

She had her differences with the South African, Gary Player. She had her differences with the PGA tour. In addition, she had her differences with the African American community for her adamant stands against prejudicial practices.

One of the ultimate heroines in African American golf is – Maggie Hathaway

- who petitioned and was at Augusta to see Lee Elder hit a shot from the first tee at the Masters in 1975
- who was able to make peace and reconciled with Gary Player
- who was able to see Tiger Woods benefit from her protests of golf courses in California
- who was able to witness the growth of her works magnified into a national movement of civil rights protests, sit ins and non-violent demonstrations

Maggie Hathaway has been given some credit for her obligations to the civil rights movement and for her dedication to the equalization of the sport of golf to all men and women in America. She was finally inducted into the National Black Golf Hall of Fame in 1994. The County Par 3 Golf Course was renamed the "Maggie Hathaway Golf Course" in her honor. The course was also designated as the initial Los Angeles County First Tee Program.

Maggie Hathaway lived her life knowing that she was an Oscar winning star in the civil rights movement of film and golf. She etched her name in these two areas when most people shied away from the responsibilities.

Her performances were one of a kind.

After all, she was – Maggie Hathaway.

Maggie Hathaway at dedication

Maggie Hathaway, at the dedication of the Maggie Hathaway Golf Course, 1993. Photograph credit: Michael Riddick, Los Angeles CA.

Maggie Hathaway & Yvonne Burke

Maggie Hathaway with former Los Angeles County Commissioner, Yvonne
B. Burke. Photograph credit: Michael Riddick, Los Angeles CA.

Althea Gibson - The Recycled Champion

"Being the first is not easy" would not be complete without including Althea Gibson. The tennis champion was reduced to poverty and shame by a miscalculation of several business ventures. She had a room full of trophies and a scrapbook of media coverage, but, no money or a steady income. The tennis world had dismissed her as a challenger on the Professional Tour to make money. Gibson was stunned that the sport she had made prominent did not consider her as worthy to be an active participant in the new money making professional tennis tour. Although, she had won the Female Athlete of the Year Award, in addition to the Frederick C. Miller Award and the Babe Didrickson Zaharias trophy.

It is amazing that she had the talent and versatility to become an actress, a vocalist, a tennis player for entertainment and a public relations person. She played a role in the movie –"Horse Soldiers" starring John Wayne and William Holden. She formed a tennis group to play during the half times for the Harlem Globetrotters and became an advertising icon for the Wonder Bread Bakery and its Tip-Top brand.

All of these adventures did not bring in the finances to sustain a comfortable life style. Althea Gibson was financially exhausted and had to find an activity to sustain her and pay off the surmounting debts. She also wanted and craved the action of the physical and person to person contact. She needed the adrenaline pumping of "I want to see your eyes when we compete" rush. After trying her hand at a myriad of challenges she chose golf as her saving grace. This sport fit her athletic abilities and the purses paid enough money to bail her out of debt if she could duplicate the prowess as the tennis athlete.

Althea Gibson was 31 years old when she tempted the gods of fate, time and golf to declare to become a professional golfer. She has to be commended for her resolve to even consider the sport of golf as a professional at that age. She became infatuated with her own press releases and the accolades of Jerry Volpe of the Englewood Golf Club and the columnist, Gene Roswell, who intimated that she was to be the next Babe Didrickson Zaharias in the golf arena.

Gibson admitted that she already had many handicaps as far as golf was concerned. Among them were age, money, equipment, club membership, professional instructions and color. In spite of these factors, Althea Gibson was to become the first African American woman to declare as a professional to play on the Ladies Professional Golf Association (LPGA) tour in 1963. She finally earned her LPGA card in 1964 and felt that she would be entitled to all of the amenities and privileges of membership.

Gibson had her ups and downs as a golfer, but she was well respected as an athlete. Gibson also encountered some animosity on the African American United Golfers Association tour which should have accepted her with open arms. Some of the women indicated that although Gibson could hit the ball over 200 yards, she did not have a short game to get the ball into the hole. The golf community had forgotten that Gibson majored in Physical Education at Florida A & M and had an excellent record in sports participation at the school. She was a tremendous basketball player, tennis player and golf player. She was an all round athlete with the talent and capabilities to win in any sport. It was by serendipity that her mentors focused on tennis during her maturation period.

She was warmly accepted by the members of the golf community. She credits Eoline Thornton (UGA), Ted Rhodes (UGA), Lee Young (UGA), Mickey Wright (LPGA), Kathy Whitworth (LPGA), Marlene Hagge (LPGA), Alice Hovey (LPGA), Julius Boros, (PGA), Walter Reably, Jimmy Devoe, Charley Brown, and Gus Salerno for getting her on track to play the game of golf to win.

It is documented that Gibson played in 171 tournaments on the Ladies Professional Golf Association tour. However, we must keep in mind that Gibson was enthralled with the game and played in any venue that was available to her. Some of her celebrity matches were played with Ann Gregory, Joe Louis, Jackie Robinson, Billy Eckstine, Ted Rhodes and others.

She also played in various United Golfers Association (UGA) tournaments and won several tournaments sponsored by local city clubs.

Gibson entered each UGA National Open Women's Championship from 1961 until she retired. Gibson did not make it to the championship round to have a chance to win the United Golfers Association National Open Women's title.

Gibson also played in many United States Golf Association (USGA) events which are listed below.

USGA Women's Open *

Year	Course	Finish	Score	To Par
1963	Kenwood Golf Club, OH	CUT	78-82=160	+14
1965	Atlantic City Country Club, NJ	CUT	83-81=164	+20
1966	Hazeltine National Golf Club, MN	T-31	79-75-81-85 =320	+32
1967	Hot Springs Golf Club, VA	CUT	76-84=160	+18
1968	Moselem Springs Golf Club, PA	39	78-77-78-78 =311	+27
1969	Scenic Hills Country Club, FL	CUT	80-80=160	+14
1970	Muskogee Country Club, OK	T-26	73-75-74-77 =299	+15
1971	Kahkwa Country Club, PA	CUT	82-81=163	+19
1973	CC of Rochester, NY	CUT	81-90=171	+25
1976	Rolling Green Country Club, PA	CUT	88-87=175	+33

USGA Women's Amateur

Year	Course	Finish	Score	To Par
1962	Country Club of Rochester, NY	T-33	Match Play Results	

(Round 2 lost to Mrs. Paul Dye Jr.)

*Tournament records reprinted with the permission of the Museum & Archives Register, U.S.G.A., Far Hills NJ

Ms. Althea Gibson is now considered a legend in African American golf history. She was an athletic icon who conquered two sports with grace, serenity and integrity. Her entry will encourage and motivate –

- An aspiring junior golfer to become an amateur for the love of the game
- A collegiate golfer to consider becoming an academic All-American and /or to pursue a professional career
- The adult woman golfer to become more proficient to join a club or enter into USGA Tournaments

Althea Gibson did not play the race card, even though she was denied entry in several tournaments. She was able to endure many negative experiences because she had developed a philosophy that – "rookies of any color are subject to abuse, because they are competing to be number one. There can be only one number one in any arena."

This is a thought that many athletes should adopt as part of their programming to compete in any sport. It is not always about the color of the skin, it is about whether you have the skill, patience and the fire to win at all costs. You can control your own destiny.

Ms. Althea Gibson finally received recognition by the African American community as a golf pioneer and was inducted, posthumously, into the African American Golfers Hall of Fame (2005) and the National Black Golf Hall of Fame (2007).

Althea Gibson & Willie Brown

Althea Gibson, the women's champion, poses with Willie Brown, the pro-champion from Houston TX, at the 9th annual North-South Golf Tournament at Miami Springs Country Club FL, February 23, 1962. Photograph credit: Corbis Photography.

3. Carrie Purnell Russell

The LPGA Master Teaching Professional

THE TEACHING PROFESSIONAL

Many people do not realize that being a "FIRST" carries an enormous amount of responsibility. One spends most of their active hours knocking down doors, performing at a high peak of activity. Then, there is the added burden of practicing the social graces each and every day. Also included is anger management control, wherein, one has to evaluate the situation and determine the risks of speaking or acting.

It is fortunate for many young people that Carrie P. Russell chose to over look all of the being the "FIRST" issues and found a sport that gave her comfort and solace for a life time.

In 1981, Carrie P. Russell was the first and only African American woman, in America, who had earned the coveted LPGA Class A membership in the Teaching Division. That was 28 years ago. Yet today, when an attempt is made to search for her name on the T & CP roster, there are no hits.

On August 16, 2009, the LPGA inducted four women into the T & CP Hall of Fame. The name of Carrie Purnell Russell is not among them. This does not bother Mrs. Russell because she is doing what she loves best – teaching the children about the sport of golf.

She shares about her love affair with golf.

I Am
Carrie P. Russell

Most African American females, during my teen and young adult life were more involved in team sports because there was no need for money or a specific place to participate. Also, we did not seek individual or dual sport activities because of racial barriers. We also lacked the financial means necessary to play individual or dual sports.

I attended the Worcester County Public Schools in Maryland. Then I graduated with a B.S. and a M.ED. degree from West Chester State University. My regular job was teaching Health and Physical Education. However, my teaching experiences were expanded to include -

First Coach, Boys Touch Football, Berlin Middle School, 1950
First Coach, Boys Basketball Team, Berlin Middle School, 1950
Coach, Girls Basketball, Worcester High School, 1950 - 54
Benjamin Banneker Jr. High School, 1954 – 60

My introduction to golf was on Thanksgiving Day, 1953 at Texas A & M University at College Station TX. Since my husband was an Airman in the United States Air Force, we found that all military personnel, including African Americans, were welcomed at the Texas A & M University golf course. The golf professional loaned us bags, clubs and balls. It took us four hours to play nine holes the first time but it was fun!

At our next duty station, Yokota Air Force Base, Japan I spent a lot of time on the driving range practicing. During the four years there, I developed a reliable swing which enabled me to play a few rounds of golf fairly consistently. In the meantime, I was the coach of the Girls Track and Field program at Yamato High School, 1961- 62. After that, I taught at the Tachikawa Jr. High School, 1962 – 64.

When we returned to the United States in 1964, I sought formal instructions and assistance through the National Golf Foundation. The Foundation held seminars for school teachers during the summer at Pine Needles Lodge and Country Club in Pinehurst, North Carolina. My golf instructors were LPGA and PGA members who at one time were touring professionals or golf teachers. I never stopped and was always looking for other African American females with whom I could play. However, I usually played with male golfers or other non-African American women.

I taught for a year at the Bruce A. Evans Jr. High School in Washington, DC, 1965 – 66, and at the Hirschi High School in Wichita Falls, Texas, 1966 – 68. In 1968, we finally returned to Dover, Delaware. I started the first golf classes for boys and girls at the Central Middle School in 1968 – 70. During my two years at Central Middle School, I went to the Maple Dale Country Club to ask the Pro for any golf clubs he might have available for my group. This was the beginning of golf in the Middle School.

From 1970 to 1972, I was also the coach of the Dover High Girls Basketball, Track and Field teams. It was through the National Golf Foundation that I was invited to become an area consultant to conduct golf clinics for high school and college teachers and their students. It was also during this time that two LPGA members suggested that I become a member of the LPGA teaching division. I completed the certification in 1971.

When I went to the Dover High School, I took the equipment and taught golf fundamentals to girls. Two boys joined and we formed the golf group. As soon as I was hired at Delaware State College, the Athletic Department decided that an additional sport was needed for males. Golf as a sport was added to the athletic program, and I was chosen as the coach. I was also the coach of Women's Basketball (1973-79).

The college purchased mats, clubs, plastic balls for indoor use and regular ball for outdoor use. The team consisted of five white males and one African American male. Several of the males had played golf at Dover High School and were enrolled at Delaware State College. No golf scholarships were awarded to these students. As fate would have it, they demonstrated what outstanding golf athletes they were by winning the Mid-Eastern Athletic Conference Championship (MEAC) in 1977. I was their coach from 1973 to 1979.

In 1975, Ray Volpe became the Commissioner of the LPGA. He decided to introduce the LPGA tour to the world and recognize the Teaching

Division. His first step was to reorganize the teachers by dividing the members into five geographical sections. The sections were to be Western, Central, Midwest, Northeast, and Southeast and each section would have its own officers to operate the organizational sectors. I received a call from the LPGA Administration to represent the Northeast section and was elected as the first President of the LPGA Northeast Teaching and Club Professionals Division. My tenure was for two years, 1976 to 1978. I later served as the "Points" Chairman for the section.

The LPGA held its Championship at the Dupont Country Club for fourteen years. The Northeast section was requested to provide a clinic for children, ages 5 to 17 years old. We would have 150 to 300 children at each golf clinic. The LPGA also started the Urban Youth Golf program in Wilmington DE. As a volunteer, I encouraged the LPGA Director to bring the program and her teachers to the Eagle Creek Course at the Dover Air Force Base. I have committed a life time to the sport of golf and have received recognition, accolades and rewards for my services –

- "Compassion and Devotion to Golf Award" which is now known as the "Carrie P. Russell Award"
- "Pathfinder Award" of the National Association for Girls and Women in Sports
- "Certificate of Recognition" from the National Golf Foundation
- "Outstanding Contributions to the PGM Golf Clinics" by Phyllis Meekins
- "Outstanding Achievements in the Sport of Golf Award" from the Delaware African American Hall of Fame

My Professional Golf Credentials are –
- Consultant for the National Golf Foundation, 1971-1979
- LPGA Teaching Professional, 1971
- LPGA Class A Professional Teaching Member, 1974
- LPGA Master Teaching Professional, 1994
- 1991 Inductee into the Afro-American Golfers Hall of Fame

It is gratifying to see that more African American women have joined the LPGA Teaching and Club Professionals Division. I am excited every time I see African American women enjoying play on any golf course. I hope that those who play will continue to coach and encourage others.

Carrie Russell

Carrie Russell is on the golf range with students. Photograph courtesy of Carrie P. Russell.

PHOTOGRAPH
GALLERY

Photographs

1. LUCY WILLAMS MITCHUM (center) WITH 1932 UGA NATIONAL OPEN WOMEN'S CONTENDERS

2. JULIA SILER, UGA NATIONAL OPEN WOMEN'S CHAMPION, 1933

3. LUCY WILLIAMS MITCHUM ON PRACTICE GREENS, 1937

4. LUCY WILLIAMS MITCHUM WITH MOVIE CELEBRITIES, 1937

5. LUCY WILLIAMS MITCHUM WITH RALPH CHILTON, 1939 UGA PRESIDENT

6. JULIA SILER AT THE "MAC" McCULLUM TOURNAMENT, 1940

7. LADIES POSE ON GOLF COURSE, 1950

8. GREEN'S LADIES GOLF CLUB, 1954

9. GREEN'S LADIES GOLF CLUB KEYSTONE TOURNAMENT, 1955

10. LORRAINE SAWYER, GREEN'S LADIES PRESIDENT, 1956

11. UNITED STATES GOLFERS ASSOCIATION LADIES TALLY SCORES, 1956

12. UNITED GOLFERS ASSOCIATION (UGA) NATIONAL OPEN RAIN DELAY, 1956

13. NATIONAL COLORED TOURNAMENT, SHADY REST GOLF CLUB, 1925

14. EXIE OCHIER, UGA NATIONAL OPEN WOMEN'S CHAMPION, 1971 & 1972

LUCY WILLIAMS MITCHUM

Lucy Mitchum & women golfers

Lucy Williams Mitchum (seated) with the 1932 UGA women championship flight contenders. L to R, Lucille McKee, Cleo Ball, Julia Siler, Marguarite Brown, Marie Jones, Ella Able, Marian McGruder. Photograph courtesy of the Julia Townes Siler Family.

JULIA SILER, UNITED GOLFERS ASSOCIATION (UGA) WOMEN'S CHAMPION, 1933

Julia Siler

Julia Siler, 1933 UGA National Open Women's Champion. Photograph courtesy of the Julia Townes Siler Family.

LUCY WILLIAMS MITCHUM ON PRACTICE GREENS, 1937

Lucy Mitchum Practice tee

Lucy Williams Mitchum, on the practice greens, 1937. Photograph courtesy of the Lucy Williams Mitchum Family.

LUCY WILLIAMS MITCHUM WITH
MOVIE CELEBRITIES, 1937

Lucy Mitchum & Celebrity women

Louise Beaver, Lucy Williams Mitchum, Hattie McDaniel, and Angela Caley, 1939. Photograph courtesy of the Lucy Williams Mitchum Family.

LUCY WILLIAMS MITCHUM WITH RALPH CHILTON, 1939 UGA PRESIDENT

Lucy Mitchum & Ralph Chilton

Lucy Williams Mitchum is with the 1939 UGA president, Ralph Chilton. Photograph courtesy of the Lucy Williams Mitchum Family.

JULIA SILER AT MAC McCULLUM TOURNAMENT, 1940

Julia Siler & tourney winners

Julia Siler, (4th from left) is with the tournament lady winners, 1940. Photograph courtesy of the Julia Townes Siler family.

LADIES POSE ON THE GOLF COURSE, 1950

Lady golfers pose on course

Left to right: Myrtle Patterson, Vernice Turner, Francis Mays and Amelia Lucas. Photograph courtesy of the David and Vernice Turner Family.

GREEN'S LADIES GOLF CLUB

Green's Ladies Golf Club

Green's Ladies Golf Club, 1954. Photograph courtesy of Mrs. Winifred Stanford.

GREEN'S LADIES GOLF CLUB

Green's Ladies Tournament

Green's Ladies Golf Club Keystone Golf Tournament, 1955. Photograph courtesy of Mrs. Winifred Stanford.

LORRAINE SAWYER

Lorraine Sawyer

Lorraine Sawyer, president of the Green Ladies Golf Club, 1956. Photograph credit: The PUTTER Magazine.

UNITED GOLFERS ASSOCIATION (UGA) LADIES TALLY SCORES, 1956

Left to right: Alma Arvin, unidentified, Ethel Funches, Gertrude Suber, Ann Gregory, Elizabeth Rice, Rhoda Fowler (standing) Lorraine Sawyer and Francis Mays. Photograph courtesy of the Wake Robin Club Archives.

UNITED GOLFERS ASSOCIATION (UGA)
NATIONAL OPEN RAIN DELAY, 1956

UGA Rain delay

Left to right: Paris Brown, Anna Mae Robinson, Marie Pittman, Lillian Frazier, Eoline Thornton (seated). Photograph Credit: The PUTTER Magazine.

WOMEN GOLFERS AT SHADY REST GOLF CLUB

Women at Shady Rest Golf Club

National Colored Tournament. 1925 Shady Rest Golf Club, Westfield, NJ. Photograph credit: Fox News Outtake A7929-7932, courtesy of the University of South Carolina Moving Image Research Collections.

EXIE SHACKELFORD-OCHIER

Exie Shackelford-Ochier

Exie Shackelford-Ochier. 1970 and 1971 United Golfers Association National Open Women's Champion. Photograph courtesy of Exie Shackelford-Ochier.

The African American Woman Golfer
Is a special person
Her determination is unequaled
Take her lead and be one of a kind
Be you

PART THREE

The Present

Dissolution and Hope

Still Searching For The LPGA Tour Card

The ultimate goal of any woman golfer is to obtain playing status on the Ladies Professional Golf Association Tour. A few African America women have tried to make it to the Ladies Professional Golf Association Tour (LPGA) and the Duramed FUTURES Tour. The attempts have been difficult, strenuous and short lived with few returns to show for the efforts. The talent is there and many have played high caliber golf on collegiate teams.

It has been 46 years since Althea Gibson made an attempt to make it to the LPGA tour. Althea Gibson was a perfect example of a person with talent who tried to survive on the LPGA Tour without a secured financial network. This former Wimbledon and U.S. Open Tennis champion held out for several years trying to establish credibility by winning a string of golf tournaments on the various tours. Her hopes were dashed without accomplishing this feat. She had to face the reality that it was not to be.

This is a dilemma because there is no structural success plan for one to follow for a career as a professional on a tour. Many have opted to pursue alternative careers. The alternative careers range in scope and personal objectives. Some have chosen to stay close to the game as a –

- LPGA or PGA minority community liaison
- Golf coach
- Minority youth program organizer
- LPGA or United States Golf Teaching Federation and Golf Professional

Others have stepped outside of the arena to pursue various career opportunities. Yet, there are women who have the stamina to try out the tour life regardless of the blockades. These women have a certain amount of boldness and courage to think that they can still focus on a career as a tour professional and work full time to pay the expenses. Some of them never give up.

Six African American women participated in the FUTURES Q-School to qualify for the 2009 season, - Shasta Averyhardt, Loretta Lyttle, Tierra Manigault, Zakiya Randall, Darlene Stowers and Paula Pearson-Tucker. Only three of them made the Q-School eligibility list and they are in the "Non-exempt F Category" - Zakiya Randall is 17 years old, Lorette Lyttle and Paula Pearson-Tucker have been there before.

These women can be identified in two categories, as the aspirant and, the petitioner. The aspirant is the college graduate or neophyte who had a stellar collegiate or high school golf career and feels that it is the right time to declare as a professional. The petitioner is the one who has been on the mini-tours for years and still have not advanced to the LPGA tour. This person is the one who wants to maintain a presence as a role model to future neophytes. This is also the person, especially for African American female golfers, who needs to provide the various avenues of support for the neophytes to prevent them from making the same insidious mistakes over and over again.

1. The Ladies Professional Golf Association (LPGA)

History will record that during the 20th century, three African American women qualified and played a few years on the LPGA tour – Althea Gibson, Renee Powell and LaRee Pearl Sugg played for years without establishing an outstanding record of tournament wins. In history, it will appear as if they were there just to be an "ethnic showcase" on the tour.

This description will be erroneous because the three women gave their hearts and souls to challenge the LPGA to open up it portals to the emerging African American woman golfer. They all won respect and honors for their mere presence on the tour. The down side of their accomplishments is that today, in the 21st century, there is not one African American woman golfer on the LPGA tour.

The LPGA governs two tours – the LPGA professional tour and the Duramed FUTURES developmental tour. There are distinct differences between the two tours, but there is one prerequisite that is common between the two – the qualifying ("Q") school. The only way to become a member of either tour is to pass the rigors of qualifying school to obtain a membership card.

The card is essential because it safe guards the tours from mediocre players who may clog up the system. In business, this mechanism is called "Quality Control."

This quality control mechanism for the LPGA tours consists of up front fees to play. A potential golf athlete is required to pay a fee for a place in the qualifying school stages, a fee for annual membership and a fee for each tournament entry.

Then if the entrant can make it through the qualifying stages and obtain a membership card, there are additional expenditures for travel, lodging, food, coach, trainer, caddy, practice facilities, etc. These prerequisite costs will definitely separate the serious athlete from the average athlete. These costs may also hinder a scrious and very talented athlete from entering the sport as a professional because of the lack of financial support.

Occasionally, an athlete may implore and receive an exemption from a sponsor to play in a tournament. The athlete shows up and is not on her game. She misses the cut on the second day with scores of 80 and 76. The experience can be an embarrassment to the tour, the golfer and the sponsor. The inadequate performance may prompt the sponsor not to give exemptions to her again or to some other fledgling golfers.

It is not the fault of the LPGA tour. The athlete must understand that the LPGA is a professional tour. The LPGA tour is in the business of providing sports entertainment at the behest of the sponsors and the fans. The tour is looking for the best of the best. Therefore, the athlete has to play like a professional. One cannot afford to shoot over par scores on a professional tour. Missing "the cut" also means no paycheck. An athlete is at a lost without the paycheck at the end of the tournament. It also means that a valuable spot was denied another player.

In 2008, the number one player on the LPGA tour earned in excess of two million dollars, and the 50th place player earned close to a half million dollars. So, the tour really wants those players who will go beyond the normal to advertise the strength of the tour. That is why an athlete has to play to win and reinforce the integrity of the tour.

The Duramed FUTURES tour is the developmental arm of the LPGA tour. Developmental means that an athlete can get their game in competitive order, learn the processes involved in travel, scheduling and competing in various venues against other top-notch players. The intent is to get the athlete ready to become a first class tournament golfer on the LPGA tour.

In 2008, the number one Duramed FUTURES tour player earned in excess of ninety-three thousand dollars and the tenth place player won thirty-three thousand dollars. The top ten players earned their membership cards and eligibility to play on the 2009 LPGA tour.

Several African American women have qualified and played on the Duramed FUTURES tour over the past seventeen years. Their performance has not been up to par for a group of women who have garnished accolades as MVP, Captain, Individual Champion, etc. of college teams, state and regional conferences. The average score of these exceptional athletes who were on the tour between 1991 and 2008, was 80 (74 – 90). Their total earnings came to less than twenty thousand dollars over the seventeen year period.

The dilemma for these players was and still is that their average golf scores are too high for tournament golf. These women were on elite college teams, i.e., Furman, Vanderbilt, University of Florida, Southern University and UCLA. They were exceptional golfers on their respective teams.

The only FUTURES tour player to achieve any monetary gain and tournament win status was LaRee Pearl Sugg. Sugg was an active member of the FUTURES tour from 1992 to 2002. Although she finally advanced to play on the LPGA tour, Sugg was not able to meet the expectations of the ultimate professional tour player. No African American woman has been a card carrying member of the LPGA tour since LaRee Pearl Sugg in 2001.

The LPGA and the Duramed FUTURES tours have become more accessible to women from all ethnic groups.

It is time that the African American athlete takes her talents to the next level to make a presence on the tour. It is time that the athlete stands at the first tee of a tournament and exude with confidence that says "here I am, this tournament is mine to win."

2. Why I Play Golf

Paula Pearson-Tucker

Why I Play Golf
by
Paula Pearson-Tucker

Since I took up the game of golf in 1994, I aspired to be the best that I could be as I had done with everything in my life. Nothing would challenge me more and alter my life as golf did.

I grew up in a neighborhood where sports were necessary. Mainly, a lot of boys and no nearby parks with organized sports. We played in the streets, in each others backyards, empty deserted lots or wherever we could compete without adult interference. I played against boys in street games like "sting-a-marie". It is a baseball like game with painful consequences for striking out. And, football not just "touch" or "flag" and if you were a girl and wanted to play you had to take a tackle like a man. This is the physical training I received in my early years. My first competitive sport was at the age of nine. After almost drowning in a pool filled with rowdy kids much like myself, I had to learn to swim. The only one who knew of my brush with death and that it was because I remember my life flashing before me as I gave in to the fact that I was dying, was the girl that pulled me to safety. A girl not much older than me and not a lifeguard had saved my life. I was forever grateful. I never spoke a word of this to anyone especially my parents for surely that would be the end of my trips to the pool. Swimming was something that I learned away from them. The only evidence of how good I was, were the many blue ribbons I would bring home, the change in my physique, hair and complexion. Even that life threatening episode had led me to compete.

I share this time in my life because this is the time that most professional golfers are in their junior golf formation. They are being groomed to be champions. I was so far from that. As kids growing up we knew nothing of golf. My dad had a set of golf clubs that sat in a corner on our front porch. I never even saw him touch those clubs my entire childhood. I remember him trying to get me to watch it with him on television and I remember thinking, "I would rather you stick needles in my eyes, better yet I'll stick them in my own eye before I watch any stupid golf." When his friend, Dennis Peat would visit they would talk golf as though my dad was some kind of player. I thought this odd, because I had never even seen him pick up those old clubs. My mother worked as a waitress at Riviera County Club in Coral Gables, Florida for many years. I remember riding with my dad to the golf course to pick her up from work because she didn't drive. It was in the 60s and we would have to go around back to get her and in all the years she worked there all I ever saw was the back of the building. I guess it was the clubhouse. I knew then that it was a place for rich white people, a place where all the black help had to use the rear entrance. That was my early exposure to golf.

I was born an athlete, but I had no interest in golf. There were plenty other sports that I had easier access that would serve to keep me well occupied all through school. In all the sports that I competed and there were many, I always welcomed opportunities to showcase how good I was and how better I could become. I realize that I actually thrived on it and I knew this early on. I have always been involved in some sport. It is this involvement that saved me from drugs, gangs, teenage pregnancy and all sorts of trouble that plagued so many others that I grew up with.

But, who could predict that late in life it would be the game of golf that would alter my life? In 1992, at a corporate outing in Tucson, Arizona I was as I refer to it "pimped" to play the game with a prospective client my investment firm was courting. Someone, and to this day I can't even remember who it was that took me to the driving range and showed me how to hold a golf club. I was given a caddie, told to smile pretty and waggle a lot then sent on my way. The experience would completely change me and my outlook of the game. I don't know if beating up grass and dropping putts from everywhere in the most beautiful place I had ever seen had anything to do with it or if I would have been as excited if I had this experience on some cow pasture, but I had to learn to play this game. I returned home to Atlanta with a new client, golf friends and a desire for a sport that just days before I had absolutely no interest.

That desire is what led me a year and a half after my brief encounter in Arizona to seek out others who played the game. I was told of a golf course not far from my house in Decatur, Georgia called Sugar Creek. As God would have it, on my very first visit just to check out the course, they were having a Ladies Day. There were over 30 women, mostly black all suited and carted up getting ready to go out and play. I never would have guessed this many women played golf and right in my back yard. I had found my Mecca. Sugar Creek is a course that is owned by Dekalb County and at the time I was there the head professional was black as was most of the clientele. This was the place where I got my love of the game from greats like Klenton Sparks, the head pro and Clifford Gay, a double amputee that played with me in pain whenever I asked him to. There were other legends like Tata Pie, George Johnson (Gigi), Bobby Strobble and Chuck Thorpe to name a few who would come through "The Creek". There was always someone there willing to teach and I was willing to learn. I spent every spare moment at Sugar Creek and my love of the game runs deep there. Within a year of my first visit, I was elected president of the women's association where I served for three years. My growth in the game was rapid because of the level of play of the Sugar Creek women and the time I put in to be as good as they were.

My interest in my career as a licensed stock broker was diminishing as was the market and my golf game was getting better. My position at the investment firm was so stressful and was affecting my health and happiness. My decision to walk away from a career that had given me and my son a comfortable life wasn't easy and is one that I never regretted doing. Even when I didn't know what direction my life would take, I always found solace in golf. Golf is what saved me through the times when I did not know how I would provide for me and my child. I always had the faith that God would bring me through and he did it with golf.

God put the spirit of golf in me and it has led me to where I am today. As a professional golfer and tour player the road has not been easy. In spite of financial aspect, it takes a lot emotionally to be on the road away from the comforts of home, your friends and family in an arena where, because of you color, you are not expected to succeed. I share a bit of my history as a glimpse into what may drive a woman to choose such a path. Sometimes it is not the path that we choose, but one that is chosen for us. I know that my life has a greater calling than making it to the LPGA and I know that I will make it if it God's will. At age 51, when most feel as though I am too old, that spirit in me says "you can do all things through Christ." God has given me a talent, has kept me strong and has given me a mission that goes beyond words. This is why I still play golf.

3. Carrie Jones

1962 United Golfers Association
National Open Women's Champion

I Am Still a Champion
by
Carrie Jones

I started playing golf in 1961 at the age of twenty-two at the Grove Park Golf Course in Jackson MS. I won my first competitive trophy at the 1961 Robert Wright Open at Fuller Park in Memphis, TN, by finishing in second place. That was my first official golf tournament, but it gave me the confidence to enter and to qualify to play in several United Golfers Association National Open Championships.

The 1962 UGA National Open Tournaments were also held at Fuller Park in Memphis, TN. The thing that I remember most about the Open is that my dream of winning a major championship had been realized. I had defeated Doris Wright for the United Golfers Association National Open Women's Championship title and trophy. I had accomplished this win in a field of approximately thirty of the best African American women golfers in the country. I have won approximately 130 tournament titles in various other cities and states since that notable time in my golf history.

When I started playing golf in the early 1960's, the doors of opportunity were closed to Black women golfers in the Deep South. Grove Park was the one and only nine hole golf course open to women of color as well as Black men in the city of Jackson, MS. Pete Brown was the pro and also my golf teacher. In order to challenge myself and play in significant golf tournaments I would have to leave Jackson and go to other cities outside of the state of Mississippi to compete with other lady golfers. We were often heckled and harassed and the subject to the "N" word. We were asked if we were playing with white balls or black balls. Many times golf balls were hit at us, our cars vandalized, and the police officers would not give us any assistance. When we would attempt to play at other courses, we were told we had a golf course at Grove Park, go play it! The civil rights bill was passed in 1964 and the doors started slowly opening.

I am a member of the Nine Iron Golf Club, the oldest Black golf club in the state of Mississippi. In 1978 my husband and I were the first Black husband and wife players to join the Pay Pointe Country Club in Brandon, MS. Being a member of a Country Club afforded me the opportunity to be the first Black woman to play in the club championship of which I have won at least ten times. I am the first Black woman to win three times in the Shady Oaks Country Club Championship. I am the first Black female to win the City Championship in Jackson, MS. The doors have now finally opened and I am trying to take advantage of the opportunities. Now at the age of 70, I am still representing with a seven handicap.

Carrie Jones

Carrie Jones, the 1962 United Golfers Association National Open Women's Champion. Photograph courtesy of Carrie Jones.

PART FOUR

The Future

THE TALENT

There is a new generation of African American female athletes interested and actively involved in the sport of golf. Their ages range from three to six years, from seven to 14 years, to under 18 years and finally to the college years of 19 to 23 years. They all have the same goal of becoming a LPGA tour professional.

The youngsters under the age of 13 years old have a tremendous work ethics when it comes to practice. This is probably due to the fact that they are supervised by a parent. Whereas, the teenager and older groups begin to gravitate toward more social activities, in lieu of a practice routine. The plus teens are also thinking about career options other than golf as a future life time commitment.

However, many of them may continue to play golf as a team sport in a high school or college physical education elective. Most often, a collegiate player may consider golf as a career if and only if there may be a promising monetary agreement within sight.

All of the age groups were introduced to the sport by a close family member. But, the continued success of the promising golfer can only be professionally nurtured when the athlete is weaned from the family and put in the hands of a professional management team.

The professional team should consist of a sports agent, a golf coach, a caddy, a physical and or mental trainer, a pristine golf facility, and sponsors who are willing to take a chance on a novice.

1. The Collegiate Realm

M. Mikell Johnson, Ph.D.

There are many outstanding African American females on the horizon in the intercollegiate golf rankings. These collegians are very talented athletes and are among the best academically. It is a mystery as to why they do not elect to make an attempt to explore the sport of golf as a career.

There may be hidden factors which could obstruct the efforts of trying to make it to the LPGA or Duramed FUTURES tours. The tours are in the business of sports entertainment. Like most businesses, the tours must make every attempt to have a profitable fiscal year. The tours want the best athletes who will play to win, delight the sponsors and entertain the public.

The bewilderment for the collegiate golfer is that there is no built in liaison for this athlete similar to the team sports like football, soccer or basketball. The national team sports professional organizations have a closer relationship with the athletic coaches, the sports agents and alumni associations to recruit the best potential athlete for the professional teams.

With golf, the athlete is more or less on its own. There are not many sports agents or commercial sponsors going to the colleges to sign up potential players to brandish their logos. The athlete has to declare as a professional and make an attempt to qualify for the professional tour. This can be a very overwhelming task to go from playing collegiate team golf to going out alone to establish a professional sports career. This predicament can cause the athlete to choose between applying for a "real" job with perks or to chase a dream on a golf course.

The plight of the rookie golfer trying to get their game on in competition can be an amazing journey to nowhere or to the top of the professional hierarchy. Althea Gibson was correct in her assessment of the plight of the rookie. She indicated that a rookie can not use any excuse for the treatment that she must endure when she enters a competitive arena.

All of the rules are the same and no one sees the color of skin, height, shape or language. The competition only sees a rookie, a newcomer, a novice who is trying to take the "number one" spot and title. And, in any given

120

sport, there can only be one "number one" victor, championship holder and money winner. So, if a rookie wants to become "number one," there is a battle to be fought to earn it. The rookie has to overcome all of the obstacles that come with the "number one" position and package. And most of all, the color of the skin, the native language, stature and other excuses have nothing to do with it. The rookie has to bring the "A game on" to execute a proficiency in the sport. The final assessment is the ability to compete and win.

The athlete can then make positive evaluations as to whether to try for the tour or to apply their academic major and obtain an established career path and play golf as a pastime. There is no more drama of "I should have or could have."

Some of the outstanding African American collegiate golfers who have had intercollegiate success during the past few years are:

Britney Alford, Hampton	Mackenzie Mack, Indiana State
Shasta Averyhardt, Jackson State	Tierra Manigault, Jackson State
Erica Battle, U. South Carolina	Sydney Mauk, Hampton
Honesty Biggers, S. C. State	Lisa Mitchell, Hampton
Vanessa Brockett, UCLA	Jocelyn Lewis, Alcorn State
Ana Brown, Ohio State	Katie Lonke, Harvard
Kimberly Brown, Yale	Danielle O'Neil, Spelman
Christina Check, Hampton	Sadena Parks, U. Washington
Amber Davis, U. Virginia	Danielle Robinson, Alabama State
Lauren Davis, Hampton	Christine Taylor, Spelman
Victoria Fallgren, Gonzaga U.	Jamie Taylor, Gannon
Kimberly Frye, Spelman	Annika Windon, Princeton
Hailey Hill, Hampton	Andia Winslow, Yale
Alyson Lawson, Hampton	Cheyenne Woods, Wake Forest
Eva Lewis, Spelman	Sara Young, Florida State

Biographic and tournament history of these golfers can be accessed online or via their college sports affiliations. Some of the outstanding individual accomplishments are:

2008 – Shasta Averyardt wins SWAC medalist award four years in a row

2008 – Sara Young wins 1st place in PGA-NMGC, independent women's category

2008 – Tierra Manigault qualifies for the 2008 and 2009 Duramed FUTURES Tour

2008 – Cheyenne Woods, earns a full golf scholarship to Wake Forest

2008 – Sadena Parks signs letter of intent to the University of Washington, placed 5th in PGA National Minority Championships

2008 – Amber Davis, San Gabriel League Player of the Year, also received the 1998 Nancy Lopez Outstanding female Award

2008 – Vanessa Brockett, UCLA, qualifies to play in the U.S. Women's Open

2007 – Mackenzie Mack, Indiana State sophomore places 3rd in PGA Minority Golf Championships

2006 – Erica Battle receives the Dinah Shore Trophy, best collegiate golfer in the nation

2004 – Kimberly Brown received a U.S.G.A golf fellowship, is now a First Tee Coordinator in Seattle WA

Soon the collegiate void will be filled with the athletes who have their priorities in order and are ready to arrive on the LPGA Tour with the talent and credentials to become the African American stars with exceptional winning records.

Shasta Averyhardt

What I Seek
By
Shasta Averyhardt

I, was born in Flint, Michigan on January 05, 1986, the daughter of Gregory Averyhardt and Maria Espinoza Averyhardt and was a bundle of joy. I was bright and energetic and by seven years old, it was somewhat obvious that I had athletic talent. I was feisty and not willing to let any one boss me around. At about eight years old I would go with my dad to the golf ball driving range and watch him hit golf balls. Well too no surprise my dad was not the only one driving golf balls. The range owner had some cut down clubs and that started the whole process.

I grew up playing in Flint's two major development programs; Flint Inner City Junior Golf Association operated by Mr. Shelton Neeley and Flint Junior Golf Association, operated by Ms. Judy Hamilton. I did very well in the Flint programs and went on to capture, the Flint Junior golf Association's Junior Championship in the summer of 2003 and runner-up in 2004. However, by the seventh grade I had developed an affinity for volleyball and was eager to compete. It was no doubt I would be a tall girl and aggressive, moreover my athleticism was really beginning to show.

Although, my dad encouraged me into taking golf lessons at the age of ten, but I stopped by twelve to play volleyball. My dad agreed to let me make my own decision, but, every time he would go to the golf practice range he would take me. One day we bumped into Ms. Judy Hamilton, the girl's golf coach for Flint Central High School, at the golf range. Ms. Hamilton wanted to see my golf swing and immediately she realized it was far ahead of any other high school girls in the city. Coach Judy, encouraged me not to give up on golf, but to play both sports. By fifteen years old, as an intensely competitive athlete I had made a name for myself as a fierce competitor in golf and a dominator in volleyball.

The area Flint Journal newspaper articles were all positive and stating, "one player stood out above the rest in city volleyball this season. In a closely fought battle for the city championship, Central High had the advantage because it had Shasta Averyhardt." "The 6-foot-1 junior middle hitter was the difference in the city tournament as the Indians went 3-0 to claim the title." Averyhardt heads the 2003 All-City team and also is Flint's sole representative on the All-Saginaw Valley Conference first team." Averyhardt led the Indians in nearly every category and was "everything you want as a player," said coach Central's Terry Harris. I had 223 kills, 75 aces, 227 digs and 90 blocks.

As the two-time captain and third-year letter winner, I also made the Saginaw Valley All-Academic team as a straight-A student. While at Flint Central I was the first as a sophomore to lead Flint Central High to a city golf championship and the first girl from a Flint school to qualify for a state tournament. I was named All-State in golf as a sophomore and junior at Flint Central High.

I left Flint Central High, as a senior transfer student, to take on suburbia Grand Blanc High School, where my one goal was to be on a more competitive golf team. The other goals were to help win the state championship and of course practice at the prestigious Warrick Hills Country Club. I was welcomed with a big smile and wide arms by the lovable Mrs. Martha Ryan, the four-time state championship girl's golf coach at Grand Blanc High. During this time I was still under the watchful eye of PGA swing guru Jack Seltzer a pro's pro in Flint Michigan.

At Grand Blanc High I was named team co-captain and through inspiration, solid league play and a first place regional win, the team headed to the state championship in East Lansing on the Michigan State course. Of course the team won the state championship and this was the start of a three-peat future series for coach Ryan's girls

By the end of high school, I had become an avid golfer and a force to deal with in girl's amateur golf in Michigan. I won titles in the summer golf tournaments; like the state of Michigan Powerbilt championship, the state Westfield PGA qualifier and the state of Michigan Independent Insurance Company qualifier.

I was always looking for improvement in my golf swing. So, my dad encouraged me to let PGA teaching professional Rick Kent of Loch Lomond in Grand Blanc Michigan, to take a look at my swing. Rick did a great job of fixing a swing problem that affected my timing at impact. He also noticed the similarities between my swing and that of Michele Wie's swing on tape, "it was eerie he said."

My new and current swing guru is Bill Baldwin, named by Golf Digest as the Best Teaching Professional in the State of Michigan. He is located at King Par Golf and has been a master professional since 1988 out of Flushing Michigan and Orlando Florida.

After much thought and travel I elected to attend Jackson State University in Jackson Mississippi to play with the girls' coach Eddie Payton. I decided that I would study and obtain a major in the field of Accounting. The scholarship was close to a full ride. The college is located in the south, and in the sun, plus the business school was very reputable.

Jackson State University always has tough competitors and is mostly first or second in the (SWAC) Southwest Athletic Conference standing. I did not waste any time making my presence known in the conference. During all of the four-consecutive years I won the ladies medalist honors in the SWAC competitions. In addition to the successful conference victories, I won five collegiate tournaments titles during my time at JSU.

After having a successful college and amateur career, I now want to take my talents and game to the next level. "My primary goal is to play on the (LPGA) Lady's Professional Golf Association Tour."

I want to become a Member of the LPGA and tour professionally throughout the country representing young women every where. My goal is to be one of the most competitive women golfer in the country today. I believe I have the ability and talent to play professional golf competitively at the highest level. Although, I do realize that I am developing my skills weekly and I must increase my proficiency to meet the challenges ahead. I am to be a champion.

Accomplishments

Collegiate Tournament Results 2004-2008

Year	Tournament Name	Golf Course	Par	Scores	Placing
2004	Ellingson Fall Classic	Waterwood National Golf Club	72	71, 76, 77	2nd
2005	Southern Miss. Lady Eagle Inv.	Canebrake Country Club	71	73, 73, 74	Tied for 7th
2005	SWAC Women's Championship	Links on the Bayou	72	77, 80	1st **Medalist**
2005	Flagler Fall Slam	World Golf Village: Slammer & Squire Golf Course	72	75, 77	Tied for 2nd
2006	SWAC Women's Championship	Dancing Rabbit Golf Club	72	69, 69	1st **Medalist**
2006	Women's Collegiate Championship	Stone Mountain Golf Club	71	77, 76	1st **Medalist**
2006	ULM Fred Marx Invitational	Bayou Desiard Country Club	72	76, 72, 73	2nd
2006	Lady Colonel Collegiate	Ellendale Country Club	72	72, 75	2nd
2006	Troy Univ. Women's Inv.	Arrowhead Country Club	72	78, 67	Tied for 2nd
2007	North/South Women's Collegiate	Jacksonville Beach Golf Club	72	73, 72	1st **Medalist**
2007	SWAC Women's Championship	Riverbend Links Golf Club	72	81, 71	1st **Medalist**
2008	Bash at the Beach	Daytona Beach Golf Club	71	68, 70	1st **Medalist**

2008	Southern Miss. Lady Eagle Inv.	Canebrake Country Club	71	71, 71	1st **Medalist**
2008	SWAC Women's Championship	Dancing Rabbit Golf Club	72	73, 76	1st **Medalist**
2008	Women's Collegiate Championship	Stone Mountain Golf Club	71	78, 81	1st **Medalist**

Summer Golf Tournaments 2005-2008

Year	Tournament Name	Golf Course	Par	Score	Placing
2005	Fidra Midwest Collegiate Series Event #2	Polo Fields Country Club	72	69, 79	1st **Medalist**
2005	GAM Women's Championship	Spring Meadows Country Club	72	74, 72 **Medalist**	1st* Won in a one-hole playoff
2006	Toledo Invitational	Detwiler Park Golf Course	71	69, 70	1st **Medalist**
2007	Michigan's Women's State Amateur	Egypt Valley Country Club	72	77, 81 Seeded 8th	Finalist Runner-Up
2007	GAM Women's Championship	Saginaw Country Club	71	75, 74	5th
2008	U.S. Women's Amateur Publinx	Erin Hills Golf Club	73	72, 78 Seeded 9th	Round of 32
2008	Michigan Women's State Amateur	Walnut Hills Country Club	72	74, 73 Stroke-Play **Medalist**	Semi-Finals

SHASTA AVERYHARDT

Shasta Averyhardt

Shasta Averyhardt. Photograph courtesy of Shasta Averyhardt.

Jocelyn Lewis

My Mission
by
Jocelyn LeNeta Lewis

I started playing the wonderful game of golf at the age of 15. It was the summer of my freshman year in high school, going into my sophomore year. My grandpa, Brad Murphy, who is still an avid golfer, introduced me to the game. At first, it was very boring to me just watching a person hit at a ball and walking towards a hole, and starting all over again. What fun was that?

It was not until I really sat down with him and listened to the meaning of the game. He explained that there was more to this game then what I saw. It was a personal game for everyone to play for themselves. I did not really understand that at first but still I was very interested in the why. I began to watch the sport on the TV with him. He knew all of the player's names and their games as well. I found this amazing and I wanted to become as knowledgeable as grandpa. It took me a while to attempt to watch it on my own. I enjoyed sharing that time with just him, and I still do until this day.

The summer of the first year of high school, my dad found out about a golf program at the local golf course in my neighborhood. This golf course is called City Park in Denver, Colorado. I still consider it my home course.

I remember the first time we pulled up to the course. It was so beautiful to me. All it had was a one level "club house," one big putting/chipping green, a parking lot, and the golf course. We never went out to play on the course. We just worked on the short game. When I say "we," I mean me and the other children in the program.

I know it was a Junior Golf program, but I cannot recall the name of it. I do however remember that I was the only girl there. That did not bother me one bit. I was never a shy child. I am still the same today. I made a couple of friends and really enjoyed my first day. I remember learning the putting stroke and having fun in the putting contest. Maybe that is why 'putting' is still my favorite part of the game. I still try to perfect it today. The program was cut short for the summer, because the golf course was shut down to rebuild what is now known as the New City Park Golf Course.

In the fall of my sophomore year, at East High School, I remember walking down the hallway and seeing a sign that stated "Do you want to join the Girls Golf Team? Meet tomorrow after school." I stood there for about 2 minutes re-reading the sign because I could not believe it. I am not sure what it was about it that I could not believe, but a part of me was excited and nervous.

I had really grown to love the sport over the summer and now this was my chance to try out for the team and really make it happen. I also knew that the two most important men in my life, my father Paul Lewis and grandfather really wanted me to pick up the sport. I thought about it that night and decided not to try out. This was based on selfish reasons and fear.

The next day, I found myself walking up the stairs after school to the meeting. I felt that God had led me there. At the meeting I met a couple of other girls who I knew from around school and the golf coach Susan Foster. She basically told us about the program and her goals. There was to be a small try out in about a week and things would go from there. When she asked how many of us had ever played the game, I was shocked to see that only two or three of the 6 or 7 girls had played, and not even a lot. Just like with their dads or for fun so that made me feel so much more comfortable. I told a couple of my friends that I would try out and told them to keep it a secret.

I decided not to tell my grandpa but, I had to tell my mom and dad because they had to sign a permission form for me. I didn't even practice before the tryouts. I figured either I would make the team or not. Plus, I was on the Student Council and was just really busy with school as well. When the tryout time came, everyone who tried out made the team. I was so excited. I was on the girl's golf team at East High School and that day definitely changed my life.

I finally told my grandpa and he was full of joy. He was more surprised at the fact that I tried out more than me making the team. That let me know that he knew I could do it, but just did not think that I wanted to do it.

During the renovations at City Park, we started practicing at a course about 10 minutes away called Park Hill Golf Course. This course was closer to my house and I practiced there everyday. My dad mentioned that I should work there and make money since I was there all the time. I was offered a job and I started working in the Nike Learning Center and on the Practice range.

Needless to say when I was not working, I was practicing. We had high school tournaments about twice a week where we played the other Denver Public schools. Some of the teams had really good girl players. At the time, it really intimidated me. These girls had been playing since they were younger and had it all down pat. The fact that I was one of the few African American girls out of all of the teams did not bother me. It actually made me want to play the game better and perfect it even more. I earned golf letters for three years and I was the captain of the team. We had a blast and I will never forget those high school memories.

Working at Park Hill during the summers was awesome. I was asked to help assist with the youth teaching program at the course and it was so much fun. I learned so much by teaching others. I would go back and practice and perfect the things I was teaching. There was a group of guys that I always hung out with or played with when I was not working. They kept me on my toes. They were so competitive with each other and I thought that was funny. I wish I would have joined in on that competitiveness because it would have helped me in the long run.

The general manager of Park Hill at the time was the late Samuel Williams. This man had such an impact on my life. I will never forget him. He taught and proved to me that African Americans do have a place in this wonderful industry. The road you may take does not matter. He was a man of knowledge and very well mannered. He would have me play and volunteer for charity tournaments so that I could meet other people that would soon help me in the future. I still keep in touch with these people and they have helped me just like he said. I remember there was a qualifying tournament for juniors to play in and to get a chance to play in the Junior Internationals at Castle Pines.

Needless to say, I played in the tournament, won it and had the chance to play with a Professional on the PGA Tour. The funny thing about it is that I do not even know how I won. I did not think that I played well but when I looked at the scoreboard, I played better than I thought. After winning the tournament, I went back to tell Mr. Williams that I had won and he was elated. He later took me down to the tournament and introduced me to the PGA Tour player that I would play with, Bryant Jobe. Mr. Jobe was amazing. There were two other junior golfers playing with me and we had such a wonderful time. We got a chance to ask Mr. Jobe questions and he told us many funny golf stories.

Two of the best memories from this experience were when I arrived to the course; I had a caddie with my name on her caddie bib. It was so unreal. She cleaned my ball, cleaned my clubs, and did all of the amazing things that caddies did for the professional golfer. I was spoiled. Secondly, walking up to the 18th hole at Castle Pines and seeing that crowd of people watching made me so nervous.

Mr. Jobe noticed my behavior and told me that no matter what, we were going to par this hole. As we approached the green we had an 8 foot putt that we had to make for par. The other two guys tried to make the putt but missed, so the pressure was on me. Mr. Jobe helped me line up the putt and read the break. He told me to take a practice stroke, relax and to keep my head down and trust it. It felt like I stood over that putt for at least ten minutes. I did exactly what he said to do and I heard the ball fall into the cup. The crowd went wild and he hugged me and said "good job."

What really made my day was when two little girls ran up to me and asked for my autograph. I over heard their mom say, "she is going to be on the Tour one day. We have to save this." The mom did not know that she was simply speaking about something that made an impact on my life. My grandpa and his friends were there to see my putt and I even got interviewed afterwards. That day was just amazing. I know that Mr. Williams was watching from heaven and still encouraging me to make my dreams, that he had helped me visualize, come true.

Although I was playing and practicing a lot, I never had my own set of golf clubs. I was using a set borrowed from my high school coach. One day, God blessed me to meet who I call an angel by the name of Virgil. I was practicing on the course after our regular school session. I saw a man staring at me from afar. My coach was at her car and I did not feel in danger, so I just continued to practice.

I then saw this man go up to my coach, say something to her, then proceed over to me. I will never forget his exact words-"If you are really serious about the game, go here (handing me a business card) and get whatever you need." He then walked away. I was in shock. I did not know that this man was going to bless me beyond measures. When my dad arrived, I told him about the incident and we just left it at that. I went home and called my grandpa and he was excited. He said that it was great because he and my grandma wanted to buy me a set anyway, so we would just go check out the shop from the card.

When we went, they were expecting me. I was fitted for a new set of starter clubs, shoes, a glove, tees and balls. I received every item that a golfer needs to get started with that day. My grandpa and I, after being so overwhelmed with joy, approached the counter to pay; we were told it was all paid for. Virgil had paid for everything already. I think my grandpa made them let him pay something because that was the type of man he is.

I was in awe of this stranger. I asked for a number or a way to contact him to thank him but he was such a mystery man to all who worked there. They did not know too much about him but he did tell them about me. They managed to find a number to reach him. I called that number for months and the phone just rang and rang.

About three years later, I was home from college and went up to practice at Park Hill Golf Course. As I was driving up, I saw Virgil. I was speechless. As I went to talk to him, I could not get my 'thank you' out. I left him for 10 seconds to run inside and get practice balls, came out and he was gone. Tears ran down my face. He is my angel sent from God. I still think about the occasion and cry. If I ever get a chance to see him again, I will not let him leave without showing my appreciation.

I graduated from high school and received a full ride scholarship to Alcorn State University in Lorman, Mississippi, where I played golf for four years. This was a wonderful experience. I played against some great players. I still keep in touch with some of them. The competition was high, within a small circle, and full of other women that looked just like me. Alcorn State's golf team had a lot of changes throughout my years of playing. We won one tournament. I believe it was my senior year at the Mississippi Valley Invitational. That was such a wonderful thing to do in my last year of playing for the college team. Although I never won any individual tournaments, I really enjoyed playing and meeting all of the other women out there, whether they were having fun, or competing to win. I wish I could have pushed my competitiveness side a lot more. Now, I play with golfers that give me a challenge, and I am getting better by doing so. If I could change one thing about my college experience, I would have taken more time to practice and to direct my attitude toward more positive motivation.

We did not have a course close to the campus and that was an issue. I met an LPGA Teaching Professional, Kathy Hestor who took me under her wings and gave me great lessons. My ability could have been greater if I had the motivation and had a strong support system.

During college, I had a chance to partake in a life changing experience. I was a summer intern for the PGA Tour for two years in a row. The first year I worked for the Arizona Golf Association and the second year I worked for "Shot Links." Both summers were awesome. Working with the Arizona Golf Association, I helped run tournaments, and lived in Arizona. With "Shot links," I had a chance to travel with the PGA Tour. I got a chance to experience the life that I wanted to be living one day.

After I graduated from college, with a BS degree in Computer Networking, I moved back home to Colorado. I lost my mother and went back to work for the City Park and Park Hill Golf Courses. I still worked on my game, but it just was not the same. The weather did not allow me to play and practice like I wanted and needed to. If my mother pushed anything in life, it was to live for your dreams, whatever they may be. She taught me to step out on faith, and trust in the ability that God blessed me with. I started to get discouraged when I moved back home because of a lot of negative thoughts. I became depressed. After my mom passed away, I cried, then buckled up and started to listen to what God was directing me to do.

Through my years of golf, I have developed a relationship with several mentors that I would go to for advice. I expressed my dream of becoming a professional on the LPGA Tour to all of them and they told me that I could not realize that dream in Colorado.

It was then that I decided to make a change in my life. At first, I still took matters into my own hands. I decided to start looking into the teaching side of golf because I thought I was getting too old to competitively play the on a Tour. I went to take a Players Ability Test (PAT) in Arizona during February of 2008. I was able to line up two job interviews while I was there. I told my self, if I got one of the jobs or even both, I would step out on faith and move. Well I got both of them, so I moved out to Arizona the next week.

When I first moved to Phoenix, I worked for the First Tee of Phoenix and Arrowhead Country Club, both of which have been very helpful to me. The two jobs allowed me the practice time and the space that I needed, and also allowed me to share my dream with others. I still was not whole with what I was doing. I knew that my ultimate dream was to be playing professional golf. I remembered one of the last conversations I had with my mother. She told me to live for God and he would direct all of my steps. I decided to do just that, and work on getting on the tour.

I currently work at the best golf course in Phoenix, Papago Golf Course, which has recently gone through an extensive renovation process. I am working in the Golf Shop under the instruction of a PGA Teaching Professional Albert Murdock, who also takes the time to give me lessons. I have had the honor of being a part of the start–up of a wonderful project, and have enjoyed every minute of it. Although, I have had a lot of experience within the industry, I have never had the chance to witness all that goes into opening a golf course. This experience has already allowed me to see what I have to look forward to in the future. I love to network and meet people, and both of these desires have been met working at this wonderful place.

My golf game is currently going very well. The weather in Arizona is amazing, and I have not come across a golf course that is not in tip-top shape. I try to practice three hours a day, and play at least twice a week. I stay focused by praying and thanking God for my life thus far. I am confident in knowing that the hardest step (stepping out on faith) has already been taken. In order to take my game to the next level, I must concentrate on living the life that I want to live, which consists of constant practice and meditation.

Since I have to work for a living, I do not get a chance to practice as much as I would like, but I do not let that stop me. I am still focused on the dream and will not let anything stop me.

I know that my journey with golf has been to prepare me for where I am going in the near future. I have had the pleasure of meeting wonderful people, teaching young people, learning the rules, seeing the inside ropes of all that it takes to run, operate and manage a golf course. By experiencing all of these things made me appreciate the game so much more, and all that comes and goes with this sport. I believe God has had me to experience these things so that I can remain humbled and never forget where I have been.

I am now ready to start living my dream and get what God has promised me. My goal is to try out for the Duramed FUTURES Tour in November of 2009. If anything is a hold back for me, it will be the financial support. But, I am still not worried about that. This is definitely a talent that God has blessed me with so I will continue to trust him with all that I have.

JOCELYN LEWIS

Jocelyn Lewis

Jocelyn L. Lewis. Photograph courtesy of Jocelyn Lewis.

Erica Battle Pressley

What Golf Did For Me
by
Erica Battle Pressley

My adventure with golf began with an introduction by my father, Eddie Battle. My first orientation took place at the age of six years old, at the Weed Hill Driving Range and Coldstream Golf Course in Irmo SC, where he sent me over the fences to fetch his golf balls

My dad was the greatest influence in my life as to me appreciating the game of golf. He passed away in September of 1998, due to complications from pneumonia, but I know my dad is always with me as I mature in life.

As I perfected my golf game from a youngster, it did not really develop until I entered Irmo High School. It was my individual golf coach, George Bryan III who inspired me. He, along with my dad, taught me the game of golf. He was my golf coach from age seven until I was 19. He knew my swing, my game, and my aspirations. He helped me with my confidence and knew I had talent. He encouraged me and guided me through the hardest times, especially at the age of 14 when my dad died. I would not have accomplished the many individual feats in golf and academics without his help. I really thank him for truly inspiring me to be the best golfer and person I can be.

It was at Irmo that I became a poster golfer and a center of attention. The many accolades include – South Carolina Female Athlete of the year, 2001

- Beth Daniel Player of the Year, 2001
- Qualified for 2 US Girls Junior Am 2000, 2001
- Qualified for the US Women's Amateur Tournament, 2002
- Qualified for the US Women's Am Public Links, 2001, 2004
- Won the AAAA State Girl's Individual title, 2001
- Member of the Irmo High School State Championship, 1998-2000

I competed against the current LPGA golfers Aree Song, Brittany Lincicome, Paula Creamer and Brittany Lang while I played on the American Junior Golf Association circuit and in 2 US Girl's Junior Ams.

I entered the University of South Carolina on a full golf scholarship and immediately participated in the highly competitive South Eastern Conference (SEC). By my sophomore year, I competed in the NCAA Regionals, and qualified on the SEC Honor Roll and as a NCAA Academic All-American.

I knew that I wanted to be on the LPGA tour since the age of seven. However, when I got into my sophomore year of college I began to realize that the tour may not be exactly what I wanted as a career choice. My goals changed and I began to reflect on decisions that would affect the rest of my life.

My mother, Daphne Battle has always been my number one supporter. I admire her for her strength and courage during the hard times. She has helped me to become a more well rounded person. She sacrificed a lot while I was in high school, which allowed me to become the best I could in sports and academics.

It is with my future husband, as my guide that I began to develop spiritually. I became more involved in community service programs at the University, such as –

- the Children's Hospital
- the Harvest Hope Food Bank
- the Ronald McDonald House
- the Adult and student tutoring
- the Toys for Tots
- the Meals on Wheels
- the Big Brothers/Big Sisters

I also became a member of the CHOICE Team (Students Athletes for Health Choices Concerning Alcohol) and, the Fellowship of Christian Athletes. I consider that my greatest contribution to the community is that I founded the "Golfing For God Ministry." As a result of my humanitarian commitments, I was selected to the SEC Good Works team which honors a female golfer for exceptional dedication to volunteer services. My life now seemed to have more balance as I continued to excel on the golf course and the classroom.

During my junior year, I was an essential member of the University of South Carolina golf team while maintaining a 4.0 GPA. In my senior year at the University of South Carolina I was co-captain of the golf team while helping to lead the team to another NCAA regional berth. I knew then that my dad would be proud of me.

In 2006, my senior year, I was awarded The Dinah Shore trophy that recognizes the best female golfer in the nation as to achievements in golf, academic success, leadership and community service. The University received a monetary grant of $10,000 in my name. I also received the University of South Carolina President's Award as a student athlete. That award meant the world to me. I was recognized as not only an outstanding student athlete, with much success on the golf course and in the classroom, but as a leader and was actively involved in my community. I was chosen for that Award out of all of the student athletes at the University of South Carolina.

I wanted to be the best college golfer and to graduate with the highest Grade Point Average (GPA) that I could achieve while playing a Division 1 sport. I accomplished my primary goals and more.

I graduated Magna Cum Laude with a 3.888 GPA and was a three time NCAA Academic All-American athlete. I was named to the President's List or Dean's List every semester of my college career. I obtained this success while pursuing a double major in Marketing and Real Estate at the USC Moore School of Business. I minored in Hotel, Restaurant and Tourism Management. I was able to obtain an excellent job at one of the most prestigious Real Estate Investment Trust (REIT) companies in the country as a financial analyst after I graduated. I firmly believe I would not have been selected for that position if I had not excelled in my sport and had not been an exceptional academic student.

I currently live in San Antonio, Texas with my husband, Dr. Gerald Pressley, who I met while we were both athletes at the University of South Carolina. He was on the track team and my team mates introduced me to him. Now, I have made a career change associated more with the sport of golf. I work for the Municipal Golf Association of San Antonio as the Director of Sales and Marketing. The Association manages all of the municipal golf courses within the San Antonio area as the "Alamo City Golf Trail." I schedule all the golf tournament events, manage the website and help with the marketing and planning.

I feel truly blessed to have moved to San Antonio and to have found an opportunity that I extremely enjoy. I plan to start competing in amateur events again in the summer of 2009.

ERICA BATTLE PRESSLEY

Erica Battle Pressley

Erica Battle Pressley, graduate of the University of South Carolina. Photograph courtesy of Erica Battle Pressley.

I am the African American Woman Golfer
I tried and I stumbled, but
I won the confidence to continue
I finished the 18th hole
I am a winner

2. The Juniors

143

TEENAGE TECHIES

What steps are to be taken if a teenager wants to pursue the sport as a career? The youngster can be enrolled in a LPGA Girls, LPGA Urban Youth Golf Program or a World Golf Federation First Tee program. All of the programs function on a first come basis and usually no fee is required. The programs use the game of golf as a "life skills" tool. The athlete is required to adhere to the nine values of coping with life – honesty, integrity, sportsmanship, respect, confidence, responsibility, perseverance, courtesy and judgment. The programs reward the youth by exposing them to the fundamentals of golf. The teens can also take a course in golf as part of the physical education program. And, possibly become part of the school golf team for the competitive experience. Or actively compete in many of the national and international tournaments designed specifically for the determined junior from age seven to eighteen.

The age of Internet Technology has made it possible to view the tournament status of youngsters before they reach the teenage level and up to eligibility for college rankings. And, there are some exciting prospects wanting to be the next Althea Gibson on the LPGA tour.

Young girls have expressed the desire to become the "new age" stars of the 21st century in the sport of golf. Now, they are the nova stars, glowing bright with brilliance, low handicap and passion. Will they make it to the LPGA Tour or will they burn out before even seeing a glimpse of the tour?

Only a consistent and outstanding winning tournament record during the next 10 to 15 years will tell.

Ginger and Robbi Howard, Bradenton Florida

The Howard sisters are considered to be the next pair of phenomenal athletes in the sport of golf comparable to Venus and Serena Williams in the sport of tennis. Their biographies and accomplishments can be viewed on their websites, gingerandrobbi.com and The Howard Sisters.com. The sites contain biographies, tournament data from the ages of three, many photographs and various commentaries. The girls can drive the ball 240 yards off of the tee. Between the two, they have won 77 out of 130 junior tournaments.

Zakiya Randall, Atlanta Georgia

The website of Zakiya is Zakiyarandall.org. Zakiya is a member of the Atlanta Junior Golf Association. Her website gives an overview of her golf, educational and community activities. She has qualified to play on the Duramed FUTURES tour for the year 2009. She has also received recognition for her civic and community services by the United States Congress and the Women's Sports Foundation.

Bria Sanders, Memphis Tennessee

The website is briasanders.org. She has a 12.6 USGA handicap and has won over 50% of her tournaments. Her accolades include the Memphis Junior Masters Champion, the Tennessee Junior Golf Association Player of the Year and the Tennessee Youth Achievement Award.

Mariah Stackhouse, Riverdale Georgia

Mariah does not have a specific website, but her sports accomplishments can be accessed online. She has been a member of the Tiger Woods Foundation Golf Team since 2002. She is the 2007 Atlanta Junior Golf Championship and the 2007 Georgia Girls Player of the Year. Mariah is also the Georgia State Women's Match Play Champion of 2008.

Blair Lewis, Las Mesa California

Blair Lewis is a freshman at the Frances Parker High School and does not have an official website. Among her golf honors are the Union-Tribune Player of the year and to be selected to play on the Hall of Champion All-Section Team in 2007.

The biography, tournament records and photographs of Jasmine Wade are available under her name on the Florida Junior Golf Tour website.

These young girls express the desire to become the "new Age" stars in the sport of golf. They all have very impressive local, regional and national junior golf records. Perhaps they will continue to be inspired to fulfill their dreams of success.

However, there are juniors like Shelley Williams, who began to actively play in high school and has not established a significant record to be presented on the South Carolina state Junior Golf Association website. However, she has a story that should be told.

Then there are the African American prodigies as exemplified by Naomi Mitchell. Naomi Mitchell is under the age of ten and has established many records in the junior golf world. She tells of her feats with a father in the military.

Shelley Williams

In The Footsteps of Charlie Sifford
by
Shelley D. Williams

I am Shelley Denir Williams and I am 16 years old. I was born in Columbia SC to Sherry and Dennis Williams. I have two older brothers, Dennis, Jr., and Martin and a younger sister Shayla. In 2009, I completed my sophomore year at Spring Valley High School, where I am a member of the golf, basketball and track & field teams. My other interests are writing, art and acting.

As far back as I can remember my parents have had me involved in some activity art, ballet, tennis, basketball and golf. Since I was tall for my age, I was able to join a mixed basketball league for boys and girls, although, I was the only girl. I soon had to learn how to really play the game and soon began to like the game. I began to train very hard. The training became more intense when I started playing AAU basketball. Our team traveled to tournaments in South Carolina, Georgia, North Carolina and Tennessee. With the skills and experience I gained, I was able to play on my middle school basketball team. I have been on my high school basketball team and also played on the golf team for the past two years. I have learned that it takes hard work, dedication and lots of support to achieve success at what ever you do.

During my basketball journey, I was playing golf casually with my dad because there was not a First Tee program in the Columbia area. Golf or golf scholarship opportunities were not widely communicated in the area.

Neither did the middle school or high school that I finally attended ever have a girls golf team. It was not until my freshman year in high school did I have access to a golf program

Although, I must confess that that my introduction to golf had nothing to do with golf clubs, balls or tees. It was the golf cart that drew me to the game. My dad would promise to let me drive the golf cart in order to get me to go to the golf course with him. In between maneuvering the cart path curves and dodging trees, he would let me attempt a few one foot putts. As the years went by, the putts got longer and then turned into swings that grew from the backyard to the driving range. My interest in golf grew until I reached my freshman year in high school.

My dad asked the athletic director, if the school had a girl's golf team. The athletic director indicated that the new gym teacher was interested in starting a girl's team. Then my dad met with the gym teacher and told her that I was her first candidate and able to play the game whenever she formed a team. The gym teacher began to search for other girl players to form the golf team.

I hold the honor of being the first African American female golfer at Spring Valley High School in its inaugural season. Holding this title came with some challenges.

After joining the team we found out that a girl with reasonable skills had an opportunity to earn scholarship assistance for college tuition. With this eye opening information, I began my journey to seriously develop my golf game. Golf season started at the beginning of the school year and basketball came after.

In my freshman year, there was one scheduling conflict because I had started playing the oboe in the middle school band. The policy is that you have to register for high school classes at the end of your last middle school year. I registered for the high school band. Since football started at the beginning of the school year in September the band was required to practice and to perform at halftime during the varsity football games. Even though I did not play a marching instrument, I was told that I had to participate. The problem was that band practice was at the same time as golf practice. My dad and I spoke with the golf coach about the possibility of a conflict. We were assured that the golf coach would speak to the band director concerning the time conflict and resolve the situation. Before the meeting with the golf coach, I would go to band practice and leave immediately to go to golf practice. After, the meeting, I began to go directly to golf practice. When the assistant band director gave me a warning that missing so many practices may have an affect on my grades I went to band practice.

The irony of it all is that at the next golf match, the golf coach and team left without me. This was the first time that I had been left behind. I called my dad at work in tears to tell him what had happened. He immediately left work to take me to the tournament and there was a confrontation between him and the coach. She indicated that she thought that I had quit the team since I was still involved in the band and basketball.

My mom and dad demanded a meeting with the athletic director concerning the incident. The athletic director listened to both sides about the situation and assured me that my position on the golf team was secure. Even though the conflict had been resolved and my status had been confirmed, it did not mean that I would be welcomed with open arms. I was tolerated. Subtle issues and slights continued throughout the year.

And, by this time the golf coach had recruited other players. Needless to say I was still the only African American player on the team. My mom and dad have been most supportive. They have encouraged me to persevere. My dad always encourages me not to let others stop me from reaching a goal that I have set for myself.

In my sophomore season, there was an additional African American player that joined the team. This did not change much for me.

All that I want to do is to represent the school that I love and to play the game as part of the team. Not to play as an outsider.

Excelling at a difficult game is hard enough but it is really hard when you are made to feel that you are not wanted or not a part of the team. I am now faced with going into my third year (2009-10) of this high school golf program. My past experiences thus far have me questioning if I want to continue to fight just to participate.

This is why meeting the World Golf Hall of Fame inductee Dr. Charlie Sifford, during the weekend of May 23 -25, 2009, at the 10th Annual Ridgewood Ladies Golf Tournament was an inspiring event for me. At the pre-tournament banquet, I listened to civic organizations, federal and local government officials speak of the courage, accomplishments and contributions of Charlie Sifford. I knew that I was a witness to history. And, when he shared his personal experiences, in some way, I was hearing a part of my experiences. He spoke of his humble beginnings, the inadvertent introduction to golf through caddying to earn money, which opened the door to the game he grew to love. He spoke of the friends that he made along the way and still enjoy today and his wife and family who supported him through it all. Even on that day it was evidenced by his son and nephew accompanying him to the event. When he spoke of obstacles and challenges that he had to confront, he spoke with a conviction that he was determined not to let anyone turn him away from his right to play the game he not only loved but had great ability to compete at. He also was open to bare his human vulnerability as he shared there were times he was concerned for his safety. What impacted me the most is that his humor, his humility and how through it all he was not bitter. He spoke honestly about what he felt about conditions for minorities in golf today. He is still continuing to be a trailblazer.

I know that I can do this. Playing basketball had already developed me into a well conditioned athlete. I am smart. The school year has just ended and I have the summer to work on getting better. My goals for the future are to go to college and perhaps play golf or basketball. I will pursue a degree in physical therapy. I hope to work for a professional team to help athletes prevent or recover from injuries.

I am thankful to my mom and dad and my extended family for encouraging me on this long journey. I also thank all of my teachers and coaches for helping me develop into the person that I am today.

Additionally, The First Tee program has been a great support in helping me to develop as a golfer and as a person. I thank Mr. Parker, Mr. Harmon and Mr. Davis for all they have done for me, my sister Shayla, and the other students at the First Tee program. I also thank the Ridgewood Ladies Golf Club and Mrs. Julia Boyd for providing me with the opportunity to meet and revere the moments with Dr. Charlie Sifford. He is to be honored for his sacrifices that made it possible for all aspiring African Americans and people of color to pursue the dreams of playing golf on the LPGA and PGA tours, and to play at golf courses across America. I thank him for his courage, character and persistence through his difficult journey. His legacy will live through those of us who follow in his foot steps. And, he has given me the courage to give the game of golf another chance in spite of the challenges that may arise in my junior year.

Shelley Williams & Charlie Sifford

Shelley Williams poses with Charlie Sifford, World Golf Hall of Fame inductee. Photograph courtesy of the Ridgewood Ladies Golf Club.

The Child Prodigy
Naomi Mitchell

A child prodigy can be defined as a first rate wonder, genius, superstar, skilled, rarity, master, expert, superior and talented person.

A child can have all of these attributes and still function in an adult world. The sport of golf allows a child to establish the facility with the clubs and the ball to display this unusual talent. The talent can be nurtured to adulthood by the right training and careful guidance. Otherwise, the child prodigy will encounter a burnout and give up the game forever.

During the reign of the United Golfers Association, there were a few African American girls who were acknowledged as prodigies. Their attachment to the sport began to wane as they grew older. They began to take interest in other activities, especially social activities related to the teen years.

Today, there are many programs and training facilities available to develop the talents of the prodigy. The prodigy is trained to the fullest potential and to focus on golf as a way of life.

One example of a current prodigy who is making an impact on the "junior girls category of under 13 year olds" is Naomi Mitchell.

I Am The Next "Golf Phenom"
By
Naomi Mitchell

My name is Naomi Mitchell and I was conceived to be the next star protoype in golf history. I am preordained to be the mover and the shaker in the history of women in the sport of golf in America and around the world. There has only been in the history of the Ladies Professional Golfer's Association (LPGA) three African Americans, and they are as follows: **Althea Gibson**, **Renee Powell**, and **LaRee Sugg**. I am in hopes and determination that I will realize that I am an addition to that short list of past African American LPGA players. It goes to show our lack of existence in the sport at the highest levels. I am preparing day after day on the practice range to be the contributing factor in changing that.

However, at the present time, I am only eight years old. I was born May 9, 2000 to Shonn and Anita Mitchell in Norfolk Virginia. My father, Shonn introduced me to the game of golf, and had envisioned that his first born would take the golf world to new heights, because she was born to play golf. He would be so taken away with the vision sometimes, that he would have to shake himself back into the current time zone. He began to teach me how to hit the ball at the age of two years old. He trained me to hit balls off the ground with irons, a sand wedge and a pitching wedge and off the tee with various other clubs such as 3-wood and Driver. He particularly focused on training me to play the game from the green back to the tee, because he always felt that to teach me properly was to teach from the simplest to the complex levels of ball striking, and not to start immediately at the complex levels of ball striking. Once I began to move on to the course, after much practice, he used the same process to put me in the middle of the fairway where I could score, and not to put me on to the adult tee boxes. I remember when I would play a Par 4 at 110 yards at age 4, and now at age 7, I am now playing Par 4's at yardages of 240 yards. I also remember when I would play Par 5's at 185 yards, and now I can play a Par-5 at 320 to 330 yards. I know what it feels like to be able to score par or better for my age, and distance base. It is all relative to where you are in age and size. As I have gotten older, stronger, and longer off the tee, he has noticed, and has progressively moved me back. I will stay focused, and before you know it, I will make it to the adult tees, and be shooting the same scores. That process has definitely taught the scoring zone of the game which is about 120 yards and in, and particularly around the green, and the putting part of the game.

My father has the amazing ability to make it easy for me to learn about how to use the tools of the game. He could show me and explain different things about the golf swing. He did it in way that made it easy for me to understand. So, in a short period of time, with practice, I could perform as he had instructed. I can drive a ball approximately 165 yards off of the tee and play par golf or better for 9 holes at this distance. My father is my caddy and mentor. His motto is that "to be a phenomenal athlete, you must put in the work, and the positive results will become apparent."

Thereafter, I have developed into a competitor to be able to enter into tournament golf events, since the age of five years old. Some of the results of his training are described below.

My first tournament was in the 2005 U.S. Kids Golf World Championships Qualifer. I finished <u>second</u> in the 2005 U.S. Kids Golf Qualifier held at the Crossing Golf Course in Richmond, Virginia. I told my father the night before the tournament that I was tournament ready. He told me after I said that, it appeared to him as though I had seen a light or something concerning being ready to play competitively. I went out and performed extremely well. I hit 6 of 9 greens and came in second place with a round of 44. I was very happy with the way I played, and was encouraged even more to go home and practice on the range, and be ready for my next tournament.

Also at the young age of five, I qualified and entered the 2005 U.S. Kids Golf World Championship held in Williamsburg, Virginia. In my first attempt at this tournament, I finished 38th in a field of 48 participants. I was very happy to get an invite into such a prestigious tournament. I was really enjoying the moment of being there at such a young age. Everyone that came up to me wanted to know how old I was. Once I told them that I was 5 years old, they all were like "wow." After the event, I realize that next year for this tournament that I would be even better and prepared to do much better.

I was able to become more focused and proceeded to play some fantastic golf at the 2005 Doral-Publix Golf Junior Golf Classic held in Miami, Florida. I took the 3rd place honors for girls under 7 years old. By the time I arrived at the Doral Publix Golf Junior Classic, I was much better at my game, and begin to hit more consistent shots. I performed well shooting rounds of 43 and 45 to finish in 3rd place. I was ready to once again get home to become even better on the range, which would help me be ready for my next tournament.

Still at the age of five years old, I finished in 7th place at the 2006 U.S. Kids Golf Regional Championship-Jekyll Island Cup held in Georgia. The yardage for the girls under 7 years old was 1100 yards for 9 holes. I felt much better about my game for this event. I arrived for my practice round, and I went out and shot a round of 1 under 35. I was ready for the start of the event. My goal for this tournament was to be in the top-three, and to qualify for the summer's U.S. Kids Golf World Championships. I was not successful in my goal, however I was encouraged about my game.

My father began to train me to concentrate on the tournaments that I would enter at the age of six during the year 2006. Our first and foremost goal was to qualify for the major tournament, U.S. Kids Golf World Championships. I worked extremely hard on the range, and was dramatically improving. I felt good about my chances for the upcoming qualifier.

I finished in first place at the U.S. Kids Golf World Championship Qualifier held at the Crossing Golf Course in Richmond, Virginia. My dad reminded me about how important this qualifier was to me. He kept me focused shot for shot, hole for hole. I was in a nice groove within my round by hitting 7 of 9 greens, and shooting a score of 40. I came to the club house to wait for all the scores to be posted, and what do you know, I found myself in my first sudden death playoff. I completed my goal of qualifying for the World Championships, by winning the tournament on the first hole of the sudden death playoff. We went home extremely happy, and eager to get to practice for the next month major championship, U.S. Kids Golf World Golf Championships.

NAOMI MITCHELL

Naomi Mitchell & 2009 Trophy

Naomi Mitchell, the 2009 U. S. Kids Golf Regional Champion of the Jekyll Island Cup, Jekyll Island GA. Photograph credit: Studio 7 Photography, Roswell, Ga.

Then, we went to the PEPSI Little People's Golf Championship held in Quincy, Illinois. I finished in a top ten category, with a 5th place finish. This was my first entry into this prestigious event, which is another major tournament. I was poised to do well at this event, however I didn't get the finish that I was looking for. I felt that, I lost many opportunities to finish much higher in the tournament.

We returned to Virginia, where I entered a 2nd U.S. Kids Golf World Championship Qualifier held in Haymarket, Virginia, at the Evergreen Country Club. We were on the top of the world when I won the first place trophy, especially in our home state of Virginia. That was a big tournament as well, because I had the second lowest score of the tournament of all age groups boys or girls from age 6 to 12. I went out on this gorgeous county club course, and shot extremely well. My game was looking ready to go for the upcoming World Championships. This was my second qualifier for that event. I went home saying to myself that, I have qualified twice for the upcoming championship.

With this win, we were more than ready for the 2006 U.S. Kids World Championship held in Pinehurst, North Carolina. I was sure that I could finish in a top ten position. I was only able to finish in 23rd place for Girls under 8 years old. My dad told me not to be disappointed, and that we would get back on the range and become better and stronger for the next tournament, and that I had to realize that I was only six years old. One six year old girl may not be able to win all of the tournaments all of the time. My dad is so great.

We had two more tournaments to enter as a six year old to complete the six tournaments for the year 2006, – The Doral-Publix Golf Junior Classic and the U.S. Kids Golf Regional, Jekyll Island Cup.

The 2006 Doral-Publix, Junior Golf Classic, held in Miami had a field of 628 players from 28 states and 42 countries. I was indeed happy to finish with a 5th place position for Girls under 7 years old.

The U.S. Kids Golf Regional Championship-Jekyll Island Cup in Georgia was another tough one, but I finished in 4th place in my age group. This was a particularly wonderful two day tournament, and during the final round of this tournament, I was in the final group with the eventual winner, Claire Hodges from Wildwood, MO. She and I had a stretch of four holes, where we both matched each other birdie for birdie. My dad states that it is the best golf he has seen from two young kids ever, in a final round. He said it definitely rivals any group of a final round at any level of golf, even on the professional tours. Furthermore, he said that going birdie for birdie four holes in a row is just rare on all levels. I look forward to more of those type of competitions, because it takes you to a new zone and challenge. I said prior to that final round that it would be a challenge, and was I right. It was so wonderful to be a part of the experience and fun.

I turned 7 years old in May 2007. Our goals were to obtain top ten finishes in the six tournaments and some top fives would be better with a few first place trophies.

The first tournament was the 2007 PEPSI Little People's Golf Championship in Quincy Illinois. I finished in 4th place for my age group. I really went to this tournament prepared to win, I felt slightly disappointed, when I didn't win this one. However, I told dad that we will become much better, and be ready for the next one. He looked at me, and said that is what I want to hear from you. Learn from each and every tournament good or bad, and you will be the better for it.

The second tournament was the 2007 U.S. Kids Golf World Championship Qualifier held in Virginia at the Crossing Golf Club in Richmond. I took the first place trophy home. I was now again in for the year's U.S. Kids Golf World Championships, I arrived at that qualifier knowing that I should win, and if not someone would have to literally take it from me. I went out and fired an extremely solid round shooting a 3-under 33. I came extremely close to my second hole in one. I was only one roll away from that. My game was feeling so automatic during that tournament.

The third tournament was the 2007 Callaway Golf Junior World Golf Championship in San Diego, California. This time, I finished in the 27th spot in the field of Girls ages 7–8 years old. I didn't have the finish that I was looking for, so I said I am ready to get back to practice, and be ready to go for the next event, which is another big major tournament.

The fourth tournament was the 2007 U.S. Kids Golf World Championship held in Pinehurst, North Carolina. This was my best finish in this tournament at 6th place of 68 players. I had been home on the range practicing, and became more comfortable with the shots I needed to hit for the tournament. I departed home for the tournament, and was ready to do well in such a big field of good players. I finished my first practice round with a 3-under par 33. I was definitely feeling good about my chance to do well, because I was playing nicely. I ended up with a first round score of 37, second round 34, and a final round of 33, to finish the tournament in sixth place. My dad and I went back over the three days, and we saw that we had made seven critical mistakes, and was out of first place by only seven strokes. Well, I will be back, and better for the year of 2008.

The next tournament was the 2007 Doral-Publix Junior Golf Classic in Miami. I was in good form and captured the first place trophy in a field of 8 stellar international players. I departed home enroute to the tournament, and I said to my parents that I am going to win the tournament. I arrived there for my first practice round three days before the tournament, and I shot a 9-hole round of 34. I felt ready to go, once the first round began. I ended up shooting a first round 33 to lead the tournament by seven. On the second, and final round I begin the first three holes two birdies and a par. Over the next six holes, I had a few missed cues, and ended the final round with a two-over 37. I won the tournament by four shots.

The sixth tournament for the year was the 2008 U.S. Kids Golf Regional Championship-Jekyll Island Cup in Georgia. Again, I was the Champion Golfer in my age group. I truly once again arrived knowing that I should do well, I was not going to settle for anything but a win, and that is exactly what I got, a win. The yardages for this event had increased by more that 400 yards, but no problem, because I had been home practicing for longer distances. I was poised and ready to do well. I shot rounds of 38 and 38 to win. I have since returned home, and am now practicing, preparing and looking forward to the majors this summer, the 2008 Callaway Junior World Golf Championships, held in San Diego, CA and the U.S. Kids Golf World Championships, held in Pinehurst, NC. I really want to win at those major tournaments.

SUMMARY OF ACHIEVEMENTS

Player:	*Naomi Angelia Mitchell*
Age at start of golf:	*2 years old*
Age at start of tournament play:	*5 years old*
USGA Handicap:	*(Not currently recorded)*
Total Tournaments:	**16**
Top Ten Finishes:	**13**
Wins:	**5**

Championships:

U.S. Kids Golf Virginia State Champion: **2006**
U.S. Kids Golf Virginia State Champion: **2007** (*two different U.S. Kids Golf, Virginia venues*)
Doral-Publix Junior Golf Classic **2007** *Champion*
U.S. Kids Golf Jekyll Island Cup **2008** *Champion*

Honors:

1st Hole-In-One (**Sep 23, 2006**); *Age* **6** *years old*
Member of the **2007**, *2nd Place, U.S. Kids Golf World Team Competition, U.S. Atlantic Region, # 2*
Selected to the **2008** *U.S. Kids Golf World Team Competition Girls Div., U.S. Atlantic Region,* **#2**
Selected to the **2008** *Tiger Woods Foundation National Junior Golf Team*
Appeared on the African American Golfer's Digest (Magazine and Webpage) Spring **2008** *issue*
Appeared on the Hampton Roads, Virginia, WTKR **3**, *Television Channel (Sports Section)*
Appeared on the Hampton Roads, Virginia, WAVY **10**, *Television Channel (Sports Section)*
Appeared in the Virginian-Pilot Newspaper, (Beacon Section) (Two different issue weeks)
Appeared in the Virginian-Pilot Newspaper, (Compass Section) (Two different tissue weeks)

Personal Bests:

1. 9-hole round score = 31 (age 6 years old) Practice round, Hampton Roads First Tee Chapter
2. 9-hole round score = 33 (age 7 years old) Tournament round, Longleaf Country Club, 2nd round, U.S. Kids Golf World Championships, Pinehurst, North Carolina
3. 9-hole round score =33 (age 7 years old) Tournament round, Doral Resort Golf and Spa, 1st round, Doral Publix Junior Golf Classic, Miami, Florida

NAOMI'S GOLF TOURNAMENTS

Tournament	Round 1	Round 2	Round 3	Total	Finished	Age
U.S. Kids Golf State Championship 2005	*46*	*N/A*	*N/A*	*46*	*2nd*	*5*
U.S. Kids Golf World Championship 2005 Williamsburg, VA	*52*	*47*	*59*	*158*	*38TH*	*5*
Doral-Publix Junior Golf Classic 2005	*43*	*45*	*N/A*	*88*	*3rd*	*5*
U.S. Kids Golf Regional Championship Jekyll Island Cup 2006	*40*	*42*	*N/A*	*82*	*7th*	*5*
U.S. Kids Golf World Championship Qualifier 2006 The Crossings Golf Club/ Richmond, VA	*40*	*N/A*	*N/A*	*40*	*1st*	*6*
Pepsi Little People's Golf Championships 2006	*39*	*35*	*N/A*	*74*	*5th*	*6*
U.S. Kids Golf World Championship Qualifier 2006 Evergreen Country Club/ Haymarket, VA	*37*	*N/A*	*N/A*	*37*	*1st*	*6*

U.S. Kids Golf World Championship 2006 Pinehurst, NC	40	40	42	122	23rd	6
Doral-Publix Junior Golf Classic 2006	49	37	N/A	86	6th	6
U.S. Kids Golf Regional Championship Jekyll Island Cup 2007	41	36	N/A	77	4th	6
Pepsi Little People's Golf Championships 2007	36	32	N/A	68	4th	7
U.S. Kids Golf World Championship Qualifier 2007 The Crossings Golf Club/ Richmond, VA	33	N/A	N/A	33	1st	7
Callaway Golf Junior World Golf Championships 2007	73	71	N/A	144	27th	7
U.S. Kids Golf World Championship 2007 Pinehurst, NC	37	34	33	104	6th	7
Doral-Publix Junior Golf Classic 2007	33	37	N/A	70	1st	7

Now my dad and I were looking forward to establishing some unique records for the 2008 golf season. At eight years old, I was ready to become the Champion Golfer in two major tournaments in the kid's golf world, which are the 2008 Callaway Golf Junior World Golf Championships, and the 2008 U.S. Kids Golf World Championships, held in San Diego, CA and Pinehurst, NC respectively. These two majors host the best kids in the world for the ages 7 to 8 age divisions. To this date, we are not aware of any African American girls winning these two events at such a young age. I am poised and ready to be the first one to do it.

I won the 2008 U.S. Kids Golf World Golf Championship at Pinehurst and tied for 8th place in the 2008 Callaway World Golf Championships. In addition to those tournaments, I claimed the 1st place winner's trophy at the 2008 Prestige Junior Golf Classic and came in 2nd place at the 2008 Doral-Publix Junior Classic

The 2009 year was also a defining year. I won the 2009 U.S. Kids Regional Championship Jekyll Island Cup and finished in 4th place at the 2009 U.S. Kids Golf World Golf Championship at Pinehurst NC.

I look forward to the challenge of the competition. Furthermore, I am looking forward to the years ahead in this great game of golf, as I continue to mature and grow as a person and player. I want to be recognized as a world-class renowned golfer in women's golf. My dad has told me to be able to do that, I must continue to work hard, and that is what I intend to do. Keep a watch out for me, as I pursue my goals in this great game of golf.

The African American Woman Golfer
Began as a dream
Today she is still in transition
But, tomorrow she will be the
Ultimate professional golfer

PART FIVE

The Dilemma

1. Trying to Make it to the LPGA Tour

What is a dilemma? A dilemma is a state of bewilderment, embarrassment, confusion, quandary, puzzlement, problem and perplexity. All of these conditions appear to describe the situation of the African American woman golfer's aspiration to attain professional status on the LPGA tour. The golf world is also in a quandary and is constantly trying to decipher the mystery as to why there are not any African American women on the LPGA professional tour.

Many people who do not know the qualifications of the tour are blaming the LPGA tour for not allowing the African American women the courtesy to play as professionals. The LPGA is not the reason for the missing golfer. The blame has to be placed on the shoulders of the African American athlete for not wanting to sacrifice the time and effort in obtaining and maintaining the elusive tour card. The blame is also applicable to the African American business community for not financially supporting the golf athlete.

There is an answer to this dilemma. Yes, African American women can and will eventually play as professionals on the LPGA tour. But, there is a process that they must complete to have that status. They must earn the tour card like every other player on the LPGA tour.

There is no sport in the world that will give an athlete the privileges of the organization, the privileges must be earned. And, it is time that the African American community begins to put up its corporate monies to finance one or more of their own. Being an African American is not a talent, it is what it is, an ethnic definition.

The honors and the glories will come only if there is a commitment of the athlete to the excellence of the talent. The athlete has to commit the time and effort to compete with the best. Mediocrity will not let the athlete rise to the top.

Golf is a sport where a person is motivated to get the ball in the hole in a specific number of strokes. It is a very interesting game in that a person can use a variety of clubs to play. The game can be played in a group or alone. Golf is a game of pursuit and anyone can learn how to play it. After some exposure to the game, one has to decide if their commitment to the game will be as a casual golfer, an obsessive golfer, an amateur golfer or a professional golfer.

Whatever the decision is it is best to remember that there are some natural athletes who take to the game readily and then there are others who have to be trained to develop a swing, a stance and mental discipline. There is a great amount of time that has to be expended when one begins to take to the game. The time has to be spent in practice, practice and more practice. Many individuals reach a stage where they can hit the ball a long distance with a beautiful swing. Then they hit the brick wall when it comes to the strategy and perseverance. They feel that they have paid their dues in development and sacrifices, but, are still waiting for the positive returns that never come.

There are no instant returns in the game of golf. One has to remain focused and continue the process over and over again until the muscle memory kicks in. Hit the driver, hit the 3-wood, hit the rescue club, hit the wedge and lastly, use the putter to get the ball in the hole. Even this process will not guarantee positive results.

There are several golfer types:

1) The casual golfer is one who plays the game as an athletic outlet. The score does not matter. If one is in school, golf as a physical education elective can be taken. A person can learn about how to use various clubs and some of the rules of the game. At least a person can gain some knowledge of how the game is played.

The ultimate score for the casual golfer is to shoot any score. But, if the casual golfer does not shoot a par score, it does not matter because the score can be adjusted with a U.S.G.A. handicap. And, the best part is that the athlete has enjoyed being outdoors among the flora and fauna on a beautiful day. Then the most enjoyable part of the round is the "nineteenth hole" (clubhouse bar) where one can wind down and have a talkative and fun time with golf buddies.

2) The obsessive golfer is a person who is the-"know-it-all" of everything about the game of golf except the U.S.G.A. rules. This person spends every available hour playing at golf and still has a questionable handicap. This can also be the person who blames anything and anyone for their poor performance on the course. It is advisable to negate this golfer category

because the person makes the game distasteful to many newcomers as well as the golf regulars.

3) The amateur golfer is one who plays golf to continue the history of the game as a sport. The format is usually match play, one opponent against another, hole for hole. This is when the true nuances and courtesies of the game are manifested. The U.S.G.A. holds several annual national tournaments available for the dedicated amateur golfers to test and exhibit their skills. The beauty of this category is that one is playing for the love of the game and sometimes even national pride. The U.S.G.A. events are open to golfers from around the world in accordance to specified handicap requirements.

4) The professional golfer is in a unique class. There is a different set of requirements for a person who wants to play competitive golf. An entrant declares herself as a professional and gives up all right to be classified as an amateur. The professional has to earn the privilege to play by qualifying through competition within the organization to receive the sanctioned membership card.

It is amazing that the golf gods try to make sure that the four types of golfers are seldom playing in the same group at the same time. The application of a timing sequence separates the good from the bad and the ugly.

The Ladies Professional Golf Association (LPGA) and the Professional Golf Association (PGA) require that contestants must enter the required sectional qualifying tournaments. A designated number of players advance into what is known as the "Final Stage of Q-School." A designated number of players, finishing with the lowest total scores, earn professional tour status for the following year.

Then, as a member, one has to play a specified number of tournaments and win enough money to maintain the membership card and all of the tour privileges. If a player performs poorly and fails to earn a designated amount of monies on the Tour, that player must return to Q-School and perform well enough in that tournament to retain her Tour membership.

Shooting "par" is no longer an option for a professional. A professional is required to shoot "under par" each day to anticipate being in the championship round or in the money on the weekend.

All organizations have an inherent "hazing" methodology to convince them that the professional has the ability and strength to uphold the principles, of the organization, under duress. When one reflects to being a baby, the process was to crawl, toddle, take a few steps, fall, get up and fall again. The victory was in the act of getting up. It was the determination and will to learn how to stand up and to walk alone that keeps one going through the process.

So what happens after an athlete has declared herself as a professional and makes it through the qualifying school? What are the problems encountered by the potential African American woman professional golfer?

Althea Gibson described the major problem is that "the money lies in shooting a score of below 70." This talented woman realized early in the game that it is not only about reaching the tour, it is about posting scores to become competitive to win. There is no way a golfer can shoot an average of 80 each round and expect to make a cut.

This is when the reality of the debt factors kicks in. The problem for the potential golf professional 'player' is that the athlete is bound to hit the brick wall of debt, unless there is a preconceived athlete – coach – sports agent triad - to obtain financial support to sustain the expenses of travel while competing in golf tournaments on a consistent basis, many of which are held internationally.

Does it really cost money to play on the tour? The answer is an emphatic, yes. If you do not have financial backing or sponsors to support the necessary travel on tour, or if players do not earn enough money on the tour, you are indeed open for a debt downward spiral. To make it on the tour is no cake walk. One does not show up like a Prima Donna and start playing on the tours. The athlete needs a solid network to overcome the hurdles of built-in professional card carrying expenses. It is understandable that these money issues are required to prevent the unheralded athletes from clogging up the system for others.

Even if players earn the playing status, they all have to come up with their own funding. The LPGA Tour does not provide funding. Players have to seek Sponsorships if they plan to pursue professional golf.

It has been suggested that the minority woman needs to take the initiative to knock on doors. Everyone needs a mentor to point the way to opportunities, introduce networks and warn of hazards along the way.

The burden of trying to become the next African American professional woman golfer is an enormous task, but to extend the legacy of the past legends is even greater.

2. The Solution

There will not only be one African American star, but a cadre of African American stars to emerge and be outstanding professionals on the LPGA tour. And, they will have an international appeal.

The actual question that should be asked is – what are they waiting for? It is important for African American women to be on the tour because they will symbolize the actualization of the dream of choosing golf as a career path.

There are so many African American women golf clubs and minority golf programs in operation today which indicate that they are interested in using golf to teach minority youth, ages 6 to 17, the fundamentals of life and to keep them from succumbing to the evils of the "streets." In addition, there are also many and varied local programs specifically available to girls to become engaged in golf as a means of social and individual development.

Youngsters and parents need to know that a junior player does not have to be a scratch golfer to earn a golf or non-golf scholarship. All a prospect needs to have is a strong desire to attend a college and play golf while at the institution.

All of the programs are reaping tremendous results. However there should be a component to focus on teaching the fundamentals of golf for the youngsters to get and maintain a job in golf related activities or pursue a career to become a professional golfer.

One of the ways a junior golfer or a promising collegiate golfer can make it to the LPGA arena is to participate in the competitive events designed specifically for them. These tournaments provide the golfer with competitions within their own age groups and present an opportunity to earn points or the coaches' attention toward golf scholarships.

Cyberspace has made it easier to obtain information about the history, availability, requirements, rankings, scholarships and contact personnel of practically every junior and collegiate golf tournament in the world.

National competition programs like the <u>First Tee</u>, <u>U.S. Kids World of Golf</u>, <u>Callaway Junior Golf</u> and <u>Pepsi Little People's Golf</u> Championships are designed, specifically for the 6 to 17 age groups. The Championships provide points and scholarships based on tournament performance. They have encouraged the parents of the participants to become more hands on involved in the golf programs.

Some additional tournaments that contribute to the golf rankings are:
<u>American Junior Golf Association</u> for youth who aspire to earn college scholarship points
<u>Future Collegians World Tour</u> for youth 11 to 18 to vie for scholarships
<u>International Junior Golf Tour</u> for exceptional junior golfers to compete worldwide
<u>PGA Junior Golf Championships</u> for youth 13 to 16
<u>PGA National Minority Golf Championships</u> for collegiate teams
<u>Teens On The Greens</u> an African American Junior golf program with a ranking system
<u>Tiger Woods Foundation Junior Golf Team</u> grants permanent exemption to the junior World Golf Championships

All of these programs have contributed to the development of the young athlete by having practice facilities and golf courses available on a daily or weekly basis. This exposure encourages athletes to hone their skills in preparation for the tournament competitions at an early age. Parents are expected to partake in the programs to be enlightened as to the processes involved in the tournament lifestyle. Then, they are fully aware of the procedures involved in tournament registration, travel, accommodations, handicaps and most of all, the rules of golf.

The family becomes a major participant in the development of the athlete in pursuing the sport of golf as a career. The family has to make the decision for the perpetuation of the dream when the athlete wants to continue after the age of seventeen.

As an aside, the parents of each junior golfer should become acquainted with the <u>PING American College Golf Guide</u>. The <u>Guide</u> is the best source for information about golf scholarships and the processes involved. Parents can also check <u>GolfStat Interactive Online</u>. This is a score conversion program to help the junior golfer project as to the tournament points needed for college. Another useful resource is the <u>National Collegiate Scholarship Association</u>. The Association is a clearing house for college athletic scholarships. An athlete can choose a sport, get recruiting information and make an appointment to be evaluated.

If the high school athlete is also an outstanding academic student, the sports department may assist in obtaining a scholarship to a school with a women's golf team.

By the sophomore or junior year of college, the athlete has some idea as to the actual rigors of playing competitive golf and the requirements to be voted as the Most Valuable Player. This is a major decision time as to the career options for the athlete.

Each college and university community has a Senior Women's Administrator (SWA). Her responsibility is to advise women athletes on academic matters and pre-professional requirements. This is the person who can advise an athlete as to the proper mechanism to utilize when the decision is made to declare as a professional.

The athlete has to realize that, as a "declared professional," the sport of golf has been chosen as the job and career path. This means that golf is the work option, not part-time, but full-time. Even if the athlete is physically and mentally capable to make the leap, it is virtually impossible to work part-time and pursue the sport as a first class playing professional.

A well organized and fully operational network must be in place to develop the potential golfer because the athlete cannot establish a golf career and maintain tour card requirements on a part-time basis. The reality of making it to the LPGA tour has to be a full commitment for the young professional. Either the tour card is maintained on an annual basis or the privileges accorded by the organization are lost.

Perhaps the collegiate environment can come up with a solution similar to the PGA Professional Golf Management (PGM) University Program. That is, to establish a program with the LPGA and African American academic and business communities to steer the candidate toward a career on the tour. The program will have a network of coaches, sports agents, financial organizations, etc., available for pre-graduation consultation as to the requirements a potential tour player will have to endure.

If the athlete elects to attempt the LPGA professional route, she would be eligible and given a one year pass on the Duramed FUTURES Tour to earn enough money within the top ten positions to obtain a LPGA membership card. If the athlete does not finish in the top ten on the FUTURES tour, she must return to the FUTURES Tour annual qualifying tournament or give up the dream. A budding athlete seldom seeks "proven advice" because the athlete is too engrossed in self adulation. However, it is suggested that a rookie should confer with other young players who aspire to turn Pro, their coaches and other golf professionals. Unfortunately for the African American female rookie, their ethnic advisors are so involved in their own careers that they do not care about an African American female; trying to make it on the LPGA Tour. They are only interested in producing another Tiger Woods, not a feminine lioness.

Another source for financial assistance and tournament advice should be sought from the myriad of African American affluent Women's Golf Club. One of the 1937 objectives of the Wake Robin Golf Club was to create a consortium of women's clubs. Since the end of the 1980's, there have been many independent women's clubs springing up all over the United States. There appears to be multiple independent units in each state in the nation. This is good in a way, but, detrimental in another aspect. As each unit is independent, their goals are overlapping and the total financial benefits are negated and diluted.

It would be an exceptional and positive financial maneuver if all the clubs were to form an African American Women's Golf Club Consortium. Each club would retain its independence and send delegates to the Consortium meetings. Each club could commit a specified amount of monies per year to build up a financial fund for potential professionals. The minimum amount each club would commit should not impact on their local programs, scholarships and charities.

The financial fund would be used to assist young women who want to attempt to make the sport of golf a career choice. The support stipulations would be for a one-time, one-year only basis. Each club would have candidate selection, support amount and voting rights as to who is eligible to receive finances from the fund.

This united effort would finally fulfill the last objective and futuristic vision of the original 13 Wake Robin Golf Club members who met in 1937.

The Sisters Across America appears to be fulfilling this objective in a way. Their mission is to provide support for minority women who wish to pursue a professional career in golf. If this group of women is willing to finance the neophyte, the candidate should repay them by making sure that they pass the Q-school rigors. So many entrants go to the Q-school and do not make the first cut. Going to Q-School is to test the strength of an athlete's game against other competitors. One cannot afford to shoot scores of 80 to 100 in Q-School and expect to play on the LPGA Tour.

The "Sisters Across America" organization has taken on an agenda that is primary to assist the neophyte in taking the first steps toward realizing a dream. The road will not be smooth, but it will be reassuring to know that a group of African American women are there for support.

Young African American women who have the desire to make it to the LPGA Tour should not accept monies from any organization unless they are confident that they are ready to achieve SUCCESS.

The real solution to the dilemma is the power of the six "P's" Program -

Positive, Patience, Practice, Pitching, Putting and Perseverance

- Positive thinking is the key in any endeavor to be fulfilled
- Patience truly is a virtue, not many have it in a crisis, just let it happen
- Practice is a discipline that has to be adhered to daily, not when you feel like it
- Pitching is a skill that is mandatory out of the trees, sand and around the greens
- Putting is also a skill that one has to hone at 20 feet and in
- Perseverance is the ability not to give up, but one must be willing to change directions when it is decision time

African American women golf hopefuls must keep in mind that there are young players from 31 countries on the LPGA/Duramed FUTURES Tours. You are not going to be given a free pass because you are an American or that you happen to be of African descent. You are the captain of your own ship which means that you have to work harder to control your own destiny

It would behoove the athlete to
constantly recall the old adage –
If you have the right attributes, and apply them wisely,
Destiny will take care of itself.

Part Six

A New Beginning

ONCE UPON A TIME WHEN THEY WERE QUEENS OF GOLF

No one seems to remember the names of the women golfers who were the Queens of African American golf. In 2030, it will 100 years since an African American woman won a title and a trophy in her initial golf tournament. The honor belongs to Marie Thompson Jones.

In 2030, it will be 74 years since an African American woman stood on the first tee box of a U.S.G.A Women's Open Championship tournament ready to compete. This accolade is earned by Ann Gregory.

In 2030, it will be 67 years since an African American woman defied all odds and declared as a professional golfer to play on the LPGA tour. Althea Gibson is the recipient of this tribute.

In 2030, it will be 47 years since an African American woman amassed 7 championship titles and trophies in the United Golfers Association Championship Opens. To date, this record has never been broken by any African American women or men. This phenomenal achievement belongs to Ethel Funches.

Now, do you recall their names? No, you do not even know who they are. They were the queens of African American golf, back in the day.

In 2030, it will be 66 years since the passage of Title VI, the Civil Rights Act of 1964. This Act was to insure the African American citizen all of the rights and privileges as an American.

In 2030, it will be 58 year since the enactment of Title IX, the equal opportunity in Education Act. This Act opened the doors to insure that women could equally participate in any sport without bias.

Now, in 2010, we are at a junction in the revolution where achievements and enactments are to merge into one celebratory event. Soon there will be as many African american women designated as professional career athletes in comparison to any other ethnic groups.

There is a growth in the number of African Americans who have caught the "fever" and are determined to break the mold. These athletes have substantial and verifiable credentials in competitive tournaments. And, their statistical records separate them from the mundane. The only aspects that are elusive in their quest for being on a tour is the lack of support from the African American local and business communities.

A phrase that is often heard is "why do you want to chase a little white ball?" As a retort, I must declare this as a definitive answer to such an asinine question – we can and do chase every other kind of ball in our search for glory, then why not chase the little white ball?

The sport of golf is no longer limited to the white country club settings of the privileged and elitists or for the "Black People Only" venues. The revolution has begun with the portals wide open and the African American women are passing through. They are passing through the gates as youngsters, collegians and women who have relinquished their careers, to take advantage of the opportunities to compete in professional golf tournaments.

In the new beginning, it is no longer one golfer pressing forward. It is now a multitude of athletes attempting to break down the barriers, to cross the hurdles, to remain committed, to achieve the ultimate status as a LPGA tour professional.

In the new beginning, there are also groups of women golf organizations that are committed to insure that the professional golf aspirants have the support that they need to reach their primary goals in the sport. We must not forget nor overlook the 'matriarchs' of African American golf. The matriarchs are the women who were involved in the United Golfers Association and are still actively involved in the sport. They are also the ones who maintain the folklore and oral history of the African American woman golfer.

Let the celebration begin. The struggle is not as severe, but, it is not over. African American women golfers have come a long way. There are candidates that have finally committed to making golf a career choice. And, they need the financial support of the African American community to establish a presence on the tours.

1. The Athletes

The twenty-first century has brought about a new beginning of hope for changes in the future for African American women in the sport of golf. The changes are evident by the fact that -

A. More golf clubs for girls are being formed in the public EL-HI school system

Young girls appear to be competing in golf tournaments as soon as they can walk because an increasing number of parents have become involved in the sport. Plus, there are special golf competitions for children, ages six to 18, to earn scholarship based on their performance. One can check their progress online to obtain data as to the number of tournaments, scoring averages, scholarship points and world rankings. The special programs are directed toward the development and training of the youth for a career athlete in the sport of golf. Some of the prime examples of African American girls are listed below. Some of these youngsters have made history by playing in state, regional and national women's golf tournaments. Also, many of them can be considered as cyberspace golf techies.

Naomi Mitchell from Virginia
Shelley Williams from South Carolina
Bria Sanders from Tennessee
Mariah Stackhouse from Georgia
Sadena Parks from Washington
Blair Lewis from California
Jasmine Wade, Ginger Howard and Robbi Howard from Florida

Naomi Mitchell

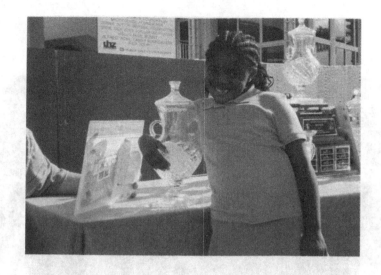

Naomi Mitchell & 2007 Trophy

Naomi Mitchell, with 2007 U.S. Kids 1st place trophy. Photograph courtesy of the Shonn Mitchell Family.

Shelley Williams

Shelley Williams

Shelley D. Williams. Photograph courtesy of the Dennis Williams Family.

B. More collegiate women have opted to declare and play as a professional on a tour

In 2005, Andia Winslow, a Yale graduate, received a sponsor's exemption to play in the Ginn's LPGA Open. She was the first African American to play in a LPGA tournament since 1995. In 2009, Cheyenne Woods, who just completed her freshman year at Wake Forest, received a sponsor's exemption to play in the Wegmans LPGA tournament. She also qualified to play in the 2009 U. S. Women's Amateur Open.

Winslow and Woods played in the LPGA tournaments as amateur invitees of the sponsor of the tournament and may or may not have another opportunity to obtain future sponsor exemptions since both of them missed the cut. But, the most positive benefit was that their presence was acknowledged and well documented throughout the Thursday and Friday television exposure. This exposure gave credence to the African American girls and women that they can and will play as a professional on the LPGA tour, one day.

Shasta Averyhardt, a product of Jackson State, declared as a professional in 2008. She prepared for the Duramed FUTURES Q-School and did not make the final cut. So, she began to hone her skills, as a professional, on a mini-tour where she would become acclimated to the trials and tribulations of being a professional, only at a minor level. She still had to play golf and bear the burden of the costs for her tournament orientations.

Her reward for the sacrifices was the first place title in a SunCoast Ladies Series tournament, held at the Stoneybrook West Golf Club on June 20, 2009. She has the courage and determination to continue to commit to the sport until she reaches her goal to play on the LPGA tour. On October 2, she finished tied for 11th place in the second LPGA, Sectional Qualifying Tournament. She is currently playing on the Duramed FUTURES Tour.

Jocelyn Lewis has been employed in the golf industry since she graduated from Alcorn State. Now, she is preparing to become involved in the competitive arena. She will be participating in a FUTURES Tour Q-school soon.

In the meantime, a former FUTURES tour athlete, Darlene Stowers, has returned to play as a professional on a fulltime basis. Stowers has a U.S.G.A. handicap of 1 and can drive over 240 yards. This time she is concentrating on the mini-tours to work her way up to the LPGA tours.

The mini-tours are often overlooked by potential professionals. A mini-golf tour is a sanctioned tour for golfers to play in competitive events for titles and prizes. The tournament scheduled season may last as long as six months or less. The cash purses are not huge, but the golfer can gain experience as how to compete in a tournament event and how to make preparations to advance to the major tours.

One mini-tour of interest is the SunCoast Ladies Series created by Mr. Scott Walker in 2007. The SunCoast Professional Golf Tour is a developmental golf tour that serves as a stepping stone for athletes whose lifelong dream is to make tournament golf their career. To learn more about the SunCoast Professional Tour and available sponsorship opportunities visit www.suncoastseries.com.

Shasta Averyhardt

Her website is <u>www.shastagolf.us</u> or one can access Meet Shasta Averyhardt or Shasta Averyhardt Golf Picture Gallery.

Shasta Averyhardt & check

Shasta Averyhardt poses with first place professional winning check. Photograph courtesy of the SunCoast Ladies Tour Series.

Jocelyn L. Lewis

Jocelyn is going to make an attempt to qualify for a professional tour in 2009. She will be leaving the safe haven of a full time job at a golf course to take a leap of faith. Her website is www.jocelynsfaithwalk.com

Jocelyn Lewis

Jocelyn Lewis is practicing her shots. Photograph courtesy of Jocelyn Lewis.

Darlene Stowers

She has developed a fund raising plan to assist her in paying for expenses. Patrons can access her website at www.darlenestowers.com and reap several personal benefits as outlined in "The Fund Raiser."

Darlene Stowers

Darlene Stowers. Photograph courtesy of Darlene Stowers.

It is good to see that several other former collegiate stars like Vanessa Brockett, Loretta Lyttle and Tierra Manigault are making their bids for a professional career in golf.

Vanessa Brockett was a child golf prodigy and graduated from UCLA. She declared as a professional in 2007, and entered the LPGA Q-school. In 2008, she qualified to play in the U.S. Women's Open. She is making preparations and will try again to make the final stage of the LPGA Q-school.

Loretta Lyttle is a graduate of U. Illinois and declared as a professional in 2007. She joined the FUTURES Tour in 2008. She also played on the SunCoast Ladies Tour and had three top 10 finishes.

Tierra Manigault was a part of the golf powerhouse at Jackson State. Manigault declared as a professional in 2008 and began to play on the FUTURES Tour.

The landscape is gradually changing as more and more African American former collegians make the declaration to become professional golfers.

2. African American Women Golf Clubs and Organizations

A new beginning has also been advanced by a special group of heroines, who are the African American women's golf clubs and organizations. Several of these groups were formed after the 50th anniversary of the Wake Robin Golf Club. The Wake Robin Golf Club is the first African American women's golf club and was established in 1937.

A few of the clubs and organizations established since 1990 are.-.
Black Jewels Ladies Golf Association, New York City NY, 2004
Ebony Golf League, OH, TX, PA, IL, 1997
Ladies at the Links, Montgomery AL, 2007
Lady Drivers, Jackson MS, 1996
Les Birdies, Cincinnati OH, 1976, 2009
Ridgewood Ladies Golf Club, Columbia SC, 1995
Sistas on the Links, Oakland CA, 2008
Sisters Across America, Orlando FL, 2006
Tee Divas & Tee Dudes, Los Angeles, CA, 1996

The following groups consented to provide information as to their purposes and roles in advancing the African American woman in the sport of golf. They represent the heroines of today and tomorrow. They are daring, adventurous and courageous. They are truly in the forefront of a new beginning of golf.

Perhaps one day, the groups will be able to pool their resources to encourage the African American business community to join them in support of the golf athletes.

Lady Drivers Golf Club (est. 1996)

The Lady Drivers Golf Club originated as a community service project of the Grove Park Duffers Golf Club in 1996. At that time, the Lady Drivers was the first African American female golf club in the state of Mississippi. Eighteen women, of all ages and professions, were organized under the leadership of Ms. Gloria S. Whitley to develop a three-fold Mission Statement. After thirteen years of growth, the Lady Drivers Golf Club has held to its missions with the following –

To learn and play the sport of golf

To expose other adults to the sport of golf

To use golf as a vehicle for community service

The Lady Drivers is the only female club on the Southern Association of Amateur Golfers Tour (SAAG), formerly known as the Southern Region "Chitlin Tour." This circuit is an organized group of African American golf clubs from the various southern states, Mississippi, Alabama, Georgia, Tennessee, Texas, Florida and Louisiana.

Though no one in the Lady Drivers is a LPGA professional, the club offers a Beginner Clinic conducted by a golf professional. This goal of the club is to raise the bar for members who desire competitive golf and to provide more opportunities for our less competitive golfers.

The club has also been very effective in the community by contributing thousands of dollars to provide children with sickle cell anemia a camp experience at "Camp Sickle Stars", The Grove Park Youth Golf Camp, Annual First Timers, Adult Male/Female Golf Clinic and the Annual Open Community Service Golf Tournament.

Contact Information

Willie Jones, President
The Lady Drivers Golf Club
POB 31128
Jackson MS 39286
www.ladydriversgolf.com.
Email – mail@ladydriversgolf.com

THE LADY DRIVERS GOLF CLUB

Lady Drivers Golf Club

The Lady Drivers Members (left to right)
Front row seated – Janice Coleman, Secretary, Willie Jones, President, Gloria Whitley, Founder & Vice president, Janessa Blackmon
Standing – Annette "Jane" Steverson, Juanita Norwood, Deborah Giles, Joyce McCants, Juanita Brown, Elizabeth Carr, Theresa Brady, Jacqueline Fleming, Financial secretary.
Members not shown – Bonnie Bunch-Glover, Carilyn Daniels, Ann Sanders, Gennia Varnado, Linda Winfield, Armerita Tell and Jo Mary Turner.
Photograph courtesy of the Lady Drivers Golf Club.

Les Birdies Golf Club, Inc. (rev. 2009)

LES BIRDIES GOLF CLUB

Les Birdies Golf Club
Photograph courtesy of the Les Birdies Golf Club.

The purposes of the Les Birdies Golf Club are –

1. To promote golf among African American females who show potential and interest in competitive golf.
2. To provide a program of organized golfing activities for its members.
3. To promote a spirit of goodwill, sportsmanship, camaraderie and solidarity among the members.
4. To provide ongoing mentoring to scholarship recipients.

Contact Information

Les Birdies Golf Club, Inc.
POB 37881
Cincinnati OH, 45222
Email – lesbirdies@lesbirdies.com
Website – www.lesbirdies.com

Ridgewood Ladies Golf Club (est. 1975)

The primary focus of the Ridgewood Ladies Golf Club is to promote the love of golf, develop great golf skills, instill leadership and civic responsibility in women throughout the community. Our secondary goals are to encourage and support the youth, and give back to our community.

The organization has donated thousands of dollars to several crucial charities. A few of the beneficiaries of our charitable nature are the "Sistercare" organization that assists battered women, the Columbia Bethlehem Center which provides diverse educational and enrichment experiences for families and several area health clinics. We actively support and sponsor young ladies who want to learn the game of golf, and also work in close association with the First Tee program in the area.

The Ridgewood Ladies Golf Club is definitely living up to its creed –

Golf Awareness
Civic Responsibility
Sportsmanship
Leadership

Contact information

Julia Boyd or Dianne Martin, Golf Committee Co-Chairs
POB 30122
Columbia SC 29230
Website – www.rlgcsc.com
Email – info@rlgcsc.com

RIDGEWOOD LADIES GOLF CLUB

Ridgewood Ladies Golf Club

Front row (left to right) – Rose Fitchett, Frances Paul, Kira Roberson, Barbara Wingate, Inez Benjamin, Pat Stephens, Val Logan, Joan Johnson, Mattie Haynes, Glenise Elmore, Teowonna Clifton
Second row – Theresa Riley, Naomi Scipio, Veronica Ramseur, Lisette Brown, Jacky Samuels, Rhonda Anderson, Linda Roberts, Roslyn Grossman, Sandra Anderson, Octavia Wade, Adrinne Gee, Julia Boyd, Carolyn Lucas, Dianne Martin

Members not pictured – Valerie Aiken, Melinda Anderson, Mary Brandyburg, Romico Caughman, Patricia Cokely, Theresa Counts-Davis, Donna Daniels, Sylvia Davis, Flora Dixon, Eva Hanna, Mary Hardy, Bernetha Henry, Marilyn Johnson, Winnie Jones, Jacqueline Lawrence, Marie Major, Shirley Price, Lynnette Robinson, Ada Simmons, Mary Starks, Diane Sumpter, Cheryl Washington, Cynthia Woodard

Ridgewood Ladies Golf Club. Photograph courtesy of the Ridgewood Ladies Golf Club.

Sisters Across America (est. 2006)

Sisters Across America, Inc. is a "not-for- profit" organization that was incorporated in Florida, in 2006, with membership across America. Our goal is to provide a professional and social network for women golfers, while raising funds to realize our mission.

The mission is to mentor and support young minority women who wish to pursue a career in professional golf. America has many junior golf programs and college golf scholarship programs, but the opportunities for support diminish greatly after college. Sisters Across America, Inc. felt that there was a need to help young minority women who want to take their golf game to the next level – a professional career in golf. One of the greatest challenges facing minority female golfers is proper training and finances to pursue their career. We want to provide the necessary support for these women.

Sisters Across America, Inc. has hosted three successful golf tournaments with participants from many states across the country. Many of these women have joined our organization in support of our mission.

Contact Information

Esther Wilson, President
POB 780005
Orlando FL 32878-0005
Website – www.sistersacrossamerica.com
Email – info@sistersacrossamerica.com

SISTERS ACROSS AMERICA, INC

Sisters Across America

Sisters Across America attendance at the 2006 Invitational held at the Orange Lake Resort, Orlando FL. Photograph courtesy of the Sisters Across America.
Photographer: Michael Dawson, Sr., Orlando FL.

Tee Divas & Tee Dudes (est.1996)

The Tee Divas Golf Club was formed in November 19996 as an outgrowth of the Western States Golf Association's Southern Area "Women in Golf Program." The founder, Doris LaCour wanted to introduce and expose more career-oriented women to the game of golf.

The continued goals of the Tee Divas Golf Club are –

- To provide members an opportunity to gain confidence in their playing skills
- T improve skills through monthly club play, clinics and regional events
- To support junior golf, scholarships, and women in golf programs
- To support a college scholarship initiative for juniors

The Tee Divas Golf Club is unique in that it is now a co-ed club that includes men who share the same desires to learn to play golf. The name of the organization was changed in 2004 to the "Tee Divas and Tee Dudes Golf Club."

Although the club travels often within the states and abroad, each member is committed to being involved in community and civic affairs. This involves becoming proactive in tournaments, fund raising, recruiting and. promoting the community action programs of the club,

Contact information

Doris LaCour, President
Website – www.teedivas-golf.com
Email – president1@teedivas-golf.com

THE TEE DIVAS AND TEE DUDES

Tee Divas & Tee Dudes Golf Club

Tee Divas & Tee Dudes Golf Club membership. Doris LaCour is the lady in front center of the photograph. Photograph courtesy of Ian Foxx and the Tee Divas and Tee Dudes Golf Club.

The African American Woman Golfer
Has always been a special breed
Her determination is unequaled
Take her lead and
Be one of a kind

Part Seven

HERSTORY

HERSTORY 1930

1930 – Marie Thompson enters and wins her 1st United Golfers Association National Open Women's Championship

1931 – Marie Thompson wins her 2nd United Golfers Association National. Open Women's Championship

1937 – The Wake Robin Golf Club is organized, on April 22, by Helen Harris. This the first African American women's golf club formed in America

1937 – The Chicago Women's Golf Club is formed by Anna Mae Black Robinson as the first club established in the Mid-western states

1938 – Cora McClinick wins the women's division of the first Intercollegiate Golf Tournament held at Tuskegee Institute

1939 – The first nine holes of Langston Golf Course are opened for play

HERSTORY 1940

1940 – The Chicago Women's Golf Club is the first all female club to host the United Golfers Association Open Championships, the National Open, the National Men's Amateur and the National Women's Amateur Opens

1941 – Cleo and Pat Ball are the first wife and husband to win the United Golfers Association National Open Pro and Women's Championship

1941 – Paris Brown is elected as the 3rd vice-president of the United Golfers Association

1941 – Margaret Brown is the first woman to win four honors at the Maryland State Open, the Murphy Cup, the Medalist prize, the Maryland State Open Cup and the John H. Murphy Trophy

1942 – Four members of the Wake Robin Golf Club, Helen Harris, Bonita Harvey, Francis Watkins and Kelly Snowden are harassed at the Fairlawn Course located in the Anacostia section of Washington DC

1944 – Geneva Wilson, Magnolia Gambrell, Frances Hill Watkins and Julia Siler are the first women to try to qualify for the Tam O'Shanter All-American Golf Tournament

1946 – Lucy Williams (Mitchum) captures the first Women's Championship in the Joe Louis Invitational

1946 – Paris Brown is named vice-president of the United Golfers Association for 1947

1946 – Lucy Williams Mitchum is the first woman to win four United Golfers Association National Open Women's Championship

1947 – Ann Gregory is first woman invited to play in the All-American Golf Tournament at the Tam O'Shanter in Chicago

1947 – Helen Harris is the first woman elected president of the Eastern Golf Association

1947 – Mae Crowder establishes the first women's golf club on the West Coast, the Vernondale Women's Golf Club

1948 – The first 9 holes of the Clearview Golf Club are opened for play

HERSTORY 1950

1953 – Mae Crowder guides the formation of the Western States Golf Association

1953 – The Vernondale Golf Club undergoes a name change to the Vernoncrest Golf Club

1954 – The Chicago Women's Golf Club sponsors the first Walter Speedy Memorial Tournament

1954 – Paris Brown is elected as the first female tournament director of the United Golfers Association

1955 – Langston Golf Course reopened with 18 holes

1956 – Ann Gregory is the first African American woman golfer to play in the United States Golf Association Women's Tournament held at the Meridian Hills Golf Club in Indianapolis IN

1959 – The National Afro-American Golfers Hall of Fame is established by Anna Robinson of the Chicago Women's Golf Club

HERSTORY 1960

1960 – Maggie Hathaway organizes the Minority Association of Golfers (MAG) to secure meaningful golf related jobs

1960 – Paris Brown is reelected to the position of tournament director and Anna Mae Robinson is the assistant director

1961 – Rhoda Fowler is the first woman to be inducted into the National Afro-American Golfers Hall of Fame

1961 – Vernice and Madelyn Turner are the first and only mother and daughter to win 1st place titles in the UGA National Open Championships

1962 – Maggie Hathaway creates the NAACP 'Image Award' to showcase people of the film industry

1963 – Althea Gibson is the first African American woman to play on the Ladies Professional Golf Association Tour (LPGA)

1964 – Title Six, the Civil Rights Act is passed

1968 – Althea Gibson publishes a book – *So Much to Live For* which tells about her adventures in life and a new found career in golf

HERSTORY 1970

1971 – Carrie Russell is the first African American to earn a Class A membership in the Ladies Professional Golf Association Teaching Division

1972 – Title Nine (IX) is enacted to ensure equality in education and sports programs for women and minorities

1973 – Ethel Funches wins her 7th United Golfers Association National Open Women's Championship

1975 – The Western States Golf Association Hall of Fame is created

1976 – Carrie Russell serves as president of the LPGA Northeast Teaching Section, from 1976 to 1978

1976 – Carrie Russell is appointed as a consultant to the National Golf Foundation

1977 – Pearl Carey is first female elected as president of the Western States Golf Association

1978 – Mae Crowder, founder of the Vernondale/Vernoncrest Golf Clubs, is the first women inducted into the Western States Golf Association Hall of Fame

1978 – The second 9-holes of the Clearview Golf Club are opened

HERSTORY 1980

1981 – Carrie Russell, 1st Class A LPGA Instructor is featured in the book – *Black Women in Sport*

1986 – The National Black Golf Hall of Fame is established

1989 – Althea Gibson is featured in the book – *I Dream a World: Portraits of Black Women Who Changed the World*

HERSTORY 1990

1990 – Debbie Adams earns LPGA Teaching & Club Professional Certification

1991 – Langston Golf Course is put on the National Register of Historic Places

1993 – The Los Angeles Par 3 Golf Course renamed the Maggie Hathaway Golf Course

1994 – Maggie Hathaway is the first woman inducted into the National Black Golf Hall of Fame

HERSTORY 2000

2000 – Nakia Davis, FUTURES Tour Golf Professional

2000 – Darlene Stowers, FUTURES Tour Golf Professional

2001 – Jean Miller Colbert wins her 15th Wake Robin Golf Club Championship

2001 – Renee' Fluker creates the Midnight Golf Program to save young people from becoming victims of the streets

2001 – LaRee Pearl Sugg, LPGA Golf Professional

2001 – The Clearview Golf Club is placed on the National Register of Historic Places

2002 – Dara Broadus, FUTURES Tour Golf Professional

2002 – Vanessa Brockett, 15 years old, wins the Los Angeles City Women's Championship

2003 – The first issue of *The African American Golfer's Digest* is published by Debert Cook

2003 – Renee Powell is honored by the Professional Golf Association with the PGA 'First Lady of Golf' Award

2003 – The Maggie Hathaway Golf Course becomes a sanctioned "First Tee" facility

2004 – The African American Golfers Hall of Fame is established

2004 – Althea Gibson's biography is published posthumously – *Born to Win: The Authorized Biography of Althea Gibson*

2004 – Addie Cobbs earns the United States Golf Federation Teaching Certification

2004 – Paula Pearson-Tucker, FUTURES Tour Golf Professional

2004 – Kimberly Brown, Yale graduate, is accepted as a U.S.G.A research intern

2005 – Naomi Mitchell, 5 years old, finished in second place at the U. S. Kids Golf World Championships Qualifier in Richmond VA

2005 – Althea Gibson is finally recognized as a golfer of note and is inducted into the African American Golfers Hall of Fame, posthumously

2005 – Felicia Brown is a Big Break contestant on the Golf Channel

2006 – Ann Gregory is inducted, posthumously, into the African American Golfers Hall of Fame

2006 – The Phyllis G. Meekins Scholarship is established by the LPGA

2006 – Naomi Mitchell. 6 years old wins the first place trophy at the U. S Kids Golf World Championships Qualifier in Richmond VA

2006 – Andia Winslow receives a sponsor's exemption to play in the Ginns LPGA Open

2006 – Wendy Boyd receives the LPGA Teaching & Club Professional certification

2007 – Althea Gibson is inducted into the National Black Golf Hall of Fame, posthumously

2007 – The Wake Robin Golf Club celebrates its 70th year anniversary

2007 – The Chicago Women's Golf Club celebrates its 70th anniversary

2007 – Barbara Douglas is named vice-president of U. S. G. A. Women's Committee

2007 – Bria Sanders, 11 years old, is selected to the Tiger Woods Foundation National Junior Golf Team for the 5th year

2007 – Sheila Johnson Newman purchases the Innisbrook PGA Championship Golf & Resort facility, Tampa, FL

2008 – Naomi Mitchell, 8 years old, is selected for the Tiger Woods Foundation Junior Golf Team

2008 – Bria Sanders, 12 years old, is named the Tennessee Player of the Year

2008 – Barbara Douglas is the first African American to chair the U. S. G. A.Women's Committee

2008 – Zakiya Randall receives the United States Congressional recognition Award

2008 – Renee Powell receives an honorary Doctorate of Laws degree conferred by St. Andrews University of Scotland

2008 – Zakiya Randall, 17 years old, qualifies to play on the Duramed FUTURES tour

2008 – Rachel Menidez, First Tee instructor at East Lake Golf Course in Atlanta, is a contestant on Big Break Michigan on the Golf Channel

2008 – Vanessa Brockett qualifies to play in the U.S. Women's Open

2008 – Loretta Lyttle qualifies to play on the Duramed FUTURES Tour

2008 – Tierra Manigault is on the Duramed FUTURES Tour roster

2009 – Paua Pearson-Tucker maintains her spot on the Duramed FUTURES Tour

2009 – *The African American Golfer's Digest*, published by Debert Cook, receives the PGA of America Diverse Supplier's Award

2009 – Cheyenne Woods receives a Wegmans exemption to play in the LPGA event

2009 – Cheyenne Woods qualifies to play in the U.S. Women's Open

2010 – Shasta Averyhardt qualifies to play on the Duramed FUTURES Tour

2010 – Paul Pearson-Tucker keeps status on the Duramed FUTURES Tour

2010 – Darlene Stowers qualifies for the Duramed FUTURES Tour

2010 – Barbara Douglas is reelected Chair, U.S.G.A. Women's Committee

Halls of Fame

HALLS OF FAME INDUCTEES

NATIONAL AFRO-AMERICAN GOLFERS HALL OF FAME, est. 1959

1961	Fowler, Rhoda	1973	Harris, Helen
1962	Robinson, Anna	1975	Williams, Ethel
1963	Brown, Paris	1976	Lawson, Eleanor
	Nelson, Jeannette	1980	Pugh, Vernette
1964	Siler, Julia	1984	Meekins, Phyllis
1966	Campbell, Mary	1986	Powell, Renee
	Gregory, Ann	1969	Funches, Ethel
1967	Williams, Agnes	1991	Carrie Russell
1971	Cowans, Thelma		

NATIONAL BLACK GOLF HALL OF FAME, est. 1986

1994	Hathaway, Maggie
2000	Coleman, Abby
2001	Young, Wilhelmenia
2003	Lee, Gladys
2006	Powell, Renee
2007	Gibson, Althea

WESTERN STATES GOLF ASSOCIATION HALL OF FAME, est. 1975

1978	Crowder, Mae	
1978	Woodyard, Mary	
1983	Fentress, Lillian	
1987	Marbury, Diane	Reason, Ella Mae
1989	Sanford, Merecdes	
1991	Carey, Pearl	Jackson, Alma
1996	Cook, Carol	
2002	Earles, Argralia	

AFRICAN AMERICAN GOLFERS HALL OF FAME, est. 2005

2005	Fluker, Renee'	Gibson, Althea
		Johnson, Selina
2006	Gould, LaJean	Gregory, Ann
		Rhodes-White, Peggy
2007	Powell, Renee	
2008	Lett, Linda	
	Broadus, Dara	
	Brown-Riley, Avis	
2009	Wake Robin Golf Club	Hon. Eleanor Holmes Norton

The Legacy

THE LEGACY

The African American woman golfer is and always will be an entity with which the sport of golf will have to contend.

The life stories of the women in this volume, were written by golfers, young and up in years who could tell about their experiences first hand. They express how the sport has had an impact on their lives. A few tell of how the sport has helped them overcome a death of a beloved mother or a father. One can not get any more personal than that.

These first hand biographies also present stories as they relate to the sport of golf in lives similar to you and me as athletes and individuals.

The women and youngsters have left as their legacies, a myriad of examples of why, how, and what to do to keep the image of the African American woman golfer alive and well in the 21st century.

A network of women has arisen who realize that this is still a journey. These women are aching for their stories to be told and are waiting for the next maverick to come along to challenge the historical system. Many women have appeared on the scene and have made the journey easier.

Please, be mindful that the joys have out weighed the negatives in this search for the African American woman golfer. It is up to each African American woman to continue the search for and to document the existence of our history as golfers.

- Please, think of them when you stand on the first tee box and hit that driver.
- Please, think of them when you hit that second shot toward the flag.
- Please, think of them, when you eagle, birdie, par or bogie the hole.
- Please, think of them when you hoist the trophy or come in last place or do not even make the cut.
- Please, do not let the history of the African American woman golfer fade away for 100 years.

I will always be seeking the history of the African American woman golfer. I leave as my legacy to the African American women golfers, two volumes of my archeological finds. As I wind down, I do pray that someone will continue to improve on the records, and include the name of every woman that has played in a golf tournament and fill the void in my efforts

Always remember that the African American woman golfer is and always will be an entity with which the world of golf will have to contend.

MMJ

Woman Golfer
The African American Woman Golfer

It is not always a level playing field
If you want to succeed
You must figure out the positives
And use them to your
Advantage

BIBLIOGRAPHY

BIBLIOGRAPHY

Acosta, R. Vivian. "The Minority Experience In Sport: Monochromatic or Technicolor." In: Cohen, Greta, ed. *Women in Sports: Issue and Controversies*. London: Sage Publications, 1993.

Baldwin, Patricia. *Remembering Early Days of Black Female Golfers*. Chicago: Go. Knight-Ridder /Tribune News Service, February 21 2001. Art # CJ7072406

Baltimore AFRO-American. *Sports Pages*. Baltimore, MD. June 1930 – December 2005: Washington Edition *Sports Pages*, 1961-2005.

Biracree, Tom. *Althea Gibson*. New York: Chelsea House Publishers, 1989.

Birrell, Susan, ed. *Women, Sport and Culture*. Champaigne IL: Human Kinetics, 1994.

Cahn, Susan K. *Coming On Strong: Gender And Sexuality In 20th Century Women's Sports*. Cambridge MA: Harvard University Press, 1994.

Chicago Defender. *Sports Pages*. Chicago, IL. June 1930 – December 2005.

Clark, Andy, and Amy Clark. *Athletic Scholarships*. New York: Checkmark Books, 2000.

Cohen, Greta .ed. *Women In Sports: Issue and Controversies*. London: Sage Publications, 1993.

Cook, Debert, ed. *The African American Golfer's Digest*. New York, 2003 - 2009

Dawkins, Marvin and Graham Kinloch. *African American Golfers During The Jim Crow Era.* Westport CN: Praegers, 2000.

Dodson, J. "A Lifetime Crusade: Maggie Hathaway's Efforts To Desegregate Golf Courses in Los Angeles." *Golf Magazine*, June 2001.

Dubois, W. E. B. *The Souls of Black Folk.* Chicago IL: Cambridge University Press, 1903.

Entine, Jon. *TABOO: Why Black Athletes Dominate Sports And Why We Are Afraid To Talk About It.* New York: Public Affairs, 2000.

Gibson, Althea. *I Always Wanted To Be Somebody.* New York: Harper, 1958.

_____. *So Much To Live For.* New York: Putnam, 1968.

Glenn, Rhonda. *The Illustrated History of Women's Golf.* New York NY: Taylor Trade Publishing, 1992.

Gray, Frances. *Born To Win: The Authorized Biography of Althea Gibson.* New York NY: John Wiley & Sons, 2004.

Johnson, M. Mikell. *The African American Woman Golfer: Her Legacy.* Westport CN. Greenwood Press, 2007.

Kennedy, John. *A Course Of Their Own: A History: Of African American Golfers.* Kansas City: Andrew McNeely Publishing, 2000.

LPGA. "History of The LPGA: 50 Years of Growth, Tradition and Excellence." http://www.lpga.com/history/content

Madden, Annette. *In Her Footsteps: 101 Remarkable Black Women From the Queen of Sheba to Queen Latifah.* New York: Gramercy Books, 2000.

McDaniel, Pete. *Uneven Lies: The Heroic Story Of African Americans In Golf* Greenwich CN: The American Golfer, 2000.

Mickey, Lisa D. "The Band Wagon Theory For Michelle Wie." http://www.duramedfuturestour.com/Blogs/Mickey

Pittsburgh Courier (New). *Sports Pages.* Pittsburgh PA: June 1930 – December 1995.

Rhoden, William C. *Forty Million Dollar Slaves.* New York NY: Crown Publishers, 2006.

Riley Richard. *"Title IX, 25 Years of Progress."* June 1997. http://wwww.ed.gov/pubs/titleIX

Robinson, Jr., Lenwood. *Skins & Grins: The Plight of Black American Golfers.* Evanston, IL: Chicago Spectrum Press, 1997.

Sinnette, Calvin. *Forbidden Fairways: African Americans And The Game Of Golf.* Chelsea MI: Sleeping Bear Press, 1998.

Smith, Lisa, ed. *Nike is a Goddess: The History of Women in Sports.* New York: Atlantic Monthly Press, 1998.

Weaver, Kathryn. The History of Langston Golf Course," June 1 2002. Washington Post.com.

Williams, Linda D. *An Analysis of American Sportswomen In Two Negro Newspapers: The Pittsburgh Courier, 1924 – 1948 and The Chicago Defender, 1932 – 1948.* Ph.D. Diss. Ohio State University, OH 1987.

THE END

INDEX

A

Able, Ella 23, 25, 26, 85
Adams, Adelaide 4
Adams, Debbie 215
Adams, Lydia 39
Afro-American Museum & Cultural
    Center xii, 17
Alford, Britney 121
American Junior Golf Association 177
Apex Golf Club 57
Arvin, Alma 6, 36, 46, 58, 95
Arvin, Juanita 61
Averyhardt, Shasta ix, xxiii, 103, 121,
    123, 124, 128, 191, 193, 218

B

Ball, Cleo 21, 26, 27, 33, 34, 39, 85,
    212
Battle, Erica. *See* Pressley, Erica
Beam, Evelyn 4
Beaver, Louise 88
Bellinger, Fettia 39
Beth Daniel Award 138
Betts, Isabell 4
Bibbs, Hazel 40
Biggers, Honesty 121
Black, Anna Mae. *See* Robinson, Anna
Black Jewels Golf 198

Blanchard, Thelma 22
Blanton, Thelma 23, 25
Bolton, Ada 23, 25
Booth, Dorothy 4
Bowman, Blanche 39
Boyd, Wendy 217
Bradley, Mildred 25, 26
Brent, Esther 26
Broadus, Dara 216, 221
Brockett, Vanessa 121, 122, 196, 216, 217
Brown, Ana 121
Brown, Felicia 216
Brown, Kimberly 121, 122, 216
Brown, Margaret 85, 213
Brown, Mary 26, 28, 34, 40, 47
Brown, Paris 6, 7, 96, 212, 213, 214, 220
Brown-Riley, Avis 221
Butkins, Mildred 27

C

Cabell, Marjorie 25
Caley, Angela 88
Callaway Golf Junior World Golf
    Championship 158
Campbell, Mary 39, 42
Carey, Pearl 215, 221
Carter, Vydie 4
Check, Christina 121

Chicago Pioneer Golf Club 23
Chicago Women's Golf Club xviii, 7, 14, 16, 21, 26, 27, 33, 39, 40, 41, 47, 58, 212, 213, 214, 217
Choi-Settes Peace Golf Club 7
Civil Rights Act 184, 214
Clearview Golf Club 213, 215, 216
Cobbs, Addie 216
Colbert, Jean Miller 6, 215
Coleman, Abby 220
Collegiate Golfers 121
Consortium 179
Cook, Carol 221
Cook, Debert xi, xvi, 216, 217, 229
Cowans, Thelma McTyre xii, xviii, 2, 20, 28, 32, 33, 34, 35, 36, 37, 40, 41, 47, 48, 58, 220
Crowder, Mae 35, 213, 215, 221

D

Davenport, Hattie 39
Davis, Aline 26
Davis, Amber 121, 122
Davis, Lauren 121
Davis, Nakia 215
Debutantes Golf Club 7
Detroit Amateurs Golf Association 24
Diggs, Bell 22
Dilemma xxii, 102, 108, 170, 180
Dinah Shore Trophy 139
Doral Publix Golf Junior Classic 155
Dorn, Pearl 22, 23
Douglas, Barbara xxii, 217, 218
Douglas Park Golf Club 23, 25, 26
Downing, Ethel 6
Duramned FUTURES Tour.
    See FUTURES Tour

E

Earles, Argralia 221
Eastern Golf Association xviii, 5, 6, 26, 47, 61, 213
Ebony Golf League 198
Ebony Ladies Golf 7

F

Fallgren, Victoria 121
Fentress, Lillian 221
Fluker, Renee' 215, 221
Ford, Myrtle 39
Foreman, Hazel 4, 6, 27, 28, 34, 46
Fowler, Rhoda 26, 95, 214, 220
Frazier, Lillian 96
Frye, Kimberly 121
Funches, Ethel xviii, 2, 6, 7, 20, 36, 45, 46, 47, 48, 49, 50, 57, 58, 59, 62, 95, 184, 214, 220
FUTURES Tour xiii, xxi, xxii, 102, 122, 135, 178, 191, 196, 215, 216, 217, 218

G

Gallery, Photograph 83
Gambrell, Magnolia 213
Garden State Dufferettes 7
Gibson, Althea xii, xx, xxiv, 62, 65, 66, 72, 73, 74, 75, 76, 102, 106, 120, 144, 153, 173, 184, 214, 215, 216, 217, 220, 221, 229, 230
Glenn, Rhonda 44, 230
Golf, Junior Programs 177
Golfer Types 171
Golfing For God 139
GolfStat Interactive 177
Goodson, Juanita 35
Gould, LaJean 221
Green's Ladies Golf Club 7, 92, 93
Gregory, Ann xii, xxiv, 2, 20, 27, 28, 34, 35, 36, 38, 39, 40, 41, 42, 43, 44, 47, 48, 58, 62, 73, 95, 184, 213, 214, 216, 220, 221
Grove, Elizabeth 23

H

Hagge, Marlene 73
Halloway, Cleo. See Ball, Cleo
Halls of Fame 44, 219, 220
Hamilton, Cookie 23, 25

Harris, Helen xii, xvii, xviii, 2, 3, 4, 6,
    7, 8, 10, 11, 212, 213, 220
Harris, Maxine 39
Harvey, Bonita 213
Hathaway, Maggie xii, xx, 35, 65, 66,
    67, 68, 69, 70, 71, 214, 215,
    216, 220, 230
Hawkins, Edith 26
HERSTORY 211, 212, 213, 214, 215,
    216, 217, 218
Hill, Hailey 121
Holland, Roberta 34
Hooks, Dorothy 39
Hovey, Alice 73
Howard, Ginger 144, 188
Howard, Robbi 144, 188
Howell, Theresa 28, 32, 34, 35, 40

I

Image Award 214

J

Jackson, Alma 221
Johnson, Anna 4, 23, 25
Johnson, Selina 217, 221
Jones, Carrie ix, xxii, 48, 113, 114, 116
Jones, Mabel 4
Jones, Marle Thompson xviii, xxiv, 2,
    20, 21, 22, 23, 24, 25, 26, 27,
    33, 85, 184, 212
Junior Golf 6, 61, 123, 130, 138, 145,
    146, 155, 157, 159, 160, 161,
    162, 163, 164, 177, 217

K

Kelly, Bernice 39

L

Ladies At The Links 198
Ladies Professional Golf Association
    (LPGA) xv, xvi, xvii, xx, xxi, xxii,
    xxiv, 45, 56, 73, 77, 78, 80, 81,
    102, 103, 105, 106, 107, 108,
    112, 118, 120, 122, 125, 133,
    134, 138, 144, 150, 153, 169,
    170, 172, 173, 176, 178, 179,
    180, 184, 185, 191, 196, 199,
    214, 215, 216, 217, 218, 230
Lady Drivers xi, 198, 199, 200
Langston Golf Course 5, 212, 213,
    215, 231
Lawson, Alyson 121
Lawson, Eleanor 220
Lee, Gladys 220
Les Birdies Golf (NC) 7
Les Birdies Golf (OH) 201, 202
Lett, Linda 221
Lewis, Blair 145, 188
Lewis, Eva 121
Lewis, Jocelyn ix, xxiii, 121, 129, 136,
    191, 194
Lincoln Golf Course 33
Logan, Vernice 46
Lonke, Katie 121
Lucas, Amelia 34, 46, 91
Lyttle, Loretta xxii, 103, 196, 217

M

Mack, Mackenzie 121, 122
Mahan, Ann 34
Manigault, Tierra xxii, 103, 121, 122,
    196, 217
Marbury, Diane 221
Mauk, Sydney 121
Mays, Frances 6, 35, 46, 91, 95
McClinick, Cora 212
McDaniel, Hattie 88
McGruder, Marian 22, 23, 25, 85
McIver, Myrtle 35
McKee, Lucille 21, 22, 23, 25, 85
McNeal, Elizabeth 6
McTyre, Thelma. *See* Cowans, Thelma
    McTyre
Meekins, Phyllis 81, 216, 220
Menidez, Rachel 217
Minority Association of Golfers 214
Mitchell, Lisa 121

Mitchell, Naomi ix, xii, xxiii, 146, 152, 153, 156, 160, 188, 189, 216, 217

Mitchum, Lucy Williams xii, xviii, 2, 20, 22, 23, 25, 26, 27, 28, 29, 30, 31, 33, 34, 36, 39, 47, 48, 84, 85, 87, 88, 89, 213

Monumental Women's Golf Auxillary 7

Morphis, Ella 39

Moye, Melnee 26

N

Nancy Lopez Award 122

National Collegiate Scholarship Association 177

Nelson, Jeannette 220

Newman, Sheila 217

Norton, Eleanor H. 221

O

Ochier, Exie Shackelford xii, 37, 42, 98

O'Neil, Danielle 121

P

Parks, Sadena 121, 122, 188

Patterson, Myrtle 58, 91

Pearson-Tucker, Paula ix, xxii, 103, 109, 110, 216

Pepsi Little People's Golf Championship 157, 158, 162, 163, 177

Photograph Gallery 83

Pierson, Laura 27

PING American College Golf Guide 177

Pioneer Golf Club 20, 23

Pittman, Marie 96

Pitts, Vivian 21, 26, 27, 39

Powell, Renee xxii, 61, 62, 106, 153, 216, 217, 220, 221

Pressley, Erica ix, xxiii, 137, 141

Proctor, Bernice 4

Professional Golf Association (PGA) xix, 172, 216

Professional Golf Management (PGM) 178

"P's" Program 180

Pugh, Vernette 220

R

Randall, Zakiya 103, 145, 217

Reason, Ella 221

Reed, Clara 34

Reid, Jerenia 4

Reynolds, Magnolia 46

Rhodes, Deborah 61

Rhodes-White, Peggy 221

Rice, Elizabeth. *See* McNeal, Elizabeth

Ridgewood Ladies Golf 149, 150, 151, 198, 203, 204

Riley, Dorcas 32, 35

Robertson, Jean 61

Robicheaux, Joylyn 39

Robinson, Anna Mae Black xviii, 2, 13, 14, 15, 16, 17, 39, 96, 212, 214, 220

Robinson, Danielle 121

Russell, Carrie ix, xi, xx, 77, 78, 79, 81, 82, 214, 215, 220

S

Sampson, Eloise 34

Sanders, Bria 145, 188, 217

Sanford, Merecdes 221

Sawyer, Lorraine 28, 34, 35, 40, 84, 94, 95

Scholarship Programs 205
  American Junior Golf Association 177
  Callaway Junior Golf 177
  First Tee 177
  Future Collegians World Tour 177
  International Junior Golf Tour 177
  Pepsi Little People's Golf 177
  PGA Junior Golf Championships 177
  PGA National Minority Golf Championships 177
  Teens On The Greens 177
  U.S. Kids World of Golf 177

Scott, Juanita 26

Senior Women's Administrator 178

Siler, Julia xi, 23, 25, 33, 84, 85, 86, 90, 213, 220
Sistas on the Links 198
Sisters Across America xi, 179, 198, 205, 206
Sixth City Golf Club 7
Skinner, Stella 4
Smith, Esther 22
Smith, Mildred 25
Smith, Sarah 6, 27, 34, 46
Snowden, Kelly 213
Solutions, Golf 175
Stackhouse, Mariah 145, 188
Stewart, Alice 35, 40
Stokien, Laurie 6, 46
Stowers, Darlene ix, xxii, 103, 191, 195, 215, 218
Suber, Gertrude 95
Sugg, LaRee Pearl 106, 108, 153, 216
SunCoast Ladies Series 191, 192

T

Tabron, Teresa 58
Taylor, Christine 121
Taylor, Jamie 121
Tee Divas & Tee Dudes 198, 207, 208
Terrell, Ethel 6, 46
Thompson, Marie. *See* Jones, Marie Thompson
Thornton, Eoline 28, 35, 40, 47, 58, 73, 96
Thoroughgood, Laura 26
Tiger Woods Foundation Junior Golf Team 177, 217
Title IX 184, 230
Turner, Madelyn ix, xi, 55, 56, 59, 61, 64, 214
Turner, Vernice ix, xi, xx, 47, 48, 55, 56, 57, 59, 60, 62, 91

U

United African American Women's Golf Club Consortium 179
United Golfers Association xi, xiii, xvii, xviii, xix, xx, xxii, 5, 6, 7, 14, 15, 16, 20, 21, 22, 23, 24, 25, 26, 27, 28, 32, 33, 34, 35, 36, 37, 39, 40, 41, 47, 48, 49, 58, 59, 61, 62, 63, 64, 73, 74, 98, 114, 116, 152, 184, 185, 212, 213, 214
Golfers Magazine 230
Women's Championships xx, 26, 40, 60, 62
United States Golf Association xii, xvii, 20, 38, 41, 74, 214

V

Vernondale/Vernoncrest Golf Club 7, 34, 35, 67, 213, 215

W

Wade, Jasmine 145, 188
Wake Robin Golf Club xi, xvii, xviii, 3, 4, 5, 6, 7, 9, 12, 45, 46, 47, 57, 58, 179, 198, 212, 213, 215, 217, 221
Walker, Jennie 23, 25
Watkins, Frances Hill 213
Whitworth, Kathy 73
Williams, Agnes 220
Williams, Ethel 4, 7, 220
Williams, Geraldine 39
Williams, Lucy. *See* Mitchum, Lucy Williams
Williams, Shelley ix, xxiii, 146, 147, 151, 188, 190
Wilson, Geneva 21, 22, 26, 39, 47, 213
Windon, Annika 121
Winslow, Andia 121, 191, 216
Women of the Sixth City Golf Club 7
Woods, Aline 27
Woods, Cheyenne 121, 122, 191, 218
Woodyard, Mary 221
Wright, Mickey 73

Y

Young, Sara 121
Young, Wilhelmenia 220

Printed in the United States
by Baker & Taylor Publisher Services